Location Matters

RECYCLING BRITAIN'S WEALTH

'The rent/land issue is the root cause of poverty ... In time, the public appropriation of rent may come to be seen not as a tax, but as the means by which the common wealth of society is collected and distributed for the benefit of all.'

(Mark Braund: *The Possibility of Progress*)

Location Matters

RECYCLING BRITAIN'S WEALTH

Tony Vickers

SHEPHEARD-WALWYN (PUBLISHERS) LTD

First published in 2007 by
Shepheard-Walwyn (Publishers) Ltd
15 Alder Road
London SW14 8ER

British Library Cataloguing in Publication Data
A catalogue record of this book
is available from the British Library

ISBN-13: 978-0-85683-251-2
ISBN-10: 0-85683-251-0

Typeset by Alacrity, Sandford, Somerset
Printed through Print Solutions, Wallington, Surrey

Contents

Acknowledgements

I AM GRATEFUL to many people and organizations for their help and encouragement in writing this: first as a discussion paper for Centre for Reform; now as a printed book. In chronological order, it was Professor Owen Connellan who first encouraged me to write on land value taxation for property professionals and, with Professor Billy McCluskey, introduced me to the Lincoln Institute of Land Policy, where Joan Youngman has remained a constant support. Together with Owen, Professor Sarah Sayce at Kingston University School of Surveying (Chair of C-SCAIPE) and Dr Munir Morad (now of South Bank University) have been my PhD supervisors for (they would say) far too long. With my Policy Delphi Group and other participants in my academic research, they have all enriched and added rigour to my work.

My friends in ALTER, especially Greg McGill – who straddles my academic, political and recreational worlds – have been invaluable in commenting on this particular creation. This project also owes a great deal to: Chris Huhne, who has championed LVT within and beyond my Party while climbing near to the top of the political 'greasy pole'; Duncan Greenland, Anthony Rowlands and the staff of CentreForum; Dave Wetzel, my opposite number in the Labour Party and ally on the 'home front' in Georgist disputes ('deep'/'shallow', full/partial, gradual/revolutionary); and Anthony Werner of Shepheard-Walwyn for taking on the publication to a tight schedule.

Detailed comment on specific parts of the book was kindly offered by: Bryan Kavanagh (Australia); Albina Aleksiene (Lithuania); Sarmite Barvika (Latvia); Andres Juss (Estonia); Josh Vincent (USA); Alanna Hartzok (UN); Dr Julie Grail (British BIDs); Peter Gibb (Scotland); Rana Roy (transport); and Iain McLean (devolution). Mavis Greenhalgh provided fresh insights with her jargon-busting proof-reading, as did my good friend and publisher Anthony Werner. However the final wording, with any errors there may be, is entirely my own.

Finally, I must thank my wife Martha for putting up with my obsession for securing property tax reform and sacrificing many weekends over the past few years, when we'd both have preferred to be enjoying the British landscape rather than my Landvaluescape.

Foreword

AS WE APPROACH the centenary of Lloyd George's 1909 People's Budget, this book is a timely reminder of one of its key themes: location matters. Despite living in a largely 'virtual' world of internet and teleconferencing, the issue of 'where' matters as much as ever and is still vital to politics, community and society. The land question has not gone away just because we don't rely on British land for Britain's food supply and industrial raw materials. Instead land lies behind the crises in affordable housing and the lack of public transport infrastructure.

Vickers combines spatial and political awareness with many years of careful academic research to give us a very competent and readable oversight of the issues surrounding land values and land value taxation. Like growing numbers of people in progressive politics, I have long believed that the behaviour of imperfect land markets needs to be addressed by modern government. Neither the property market nor the tax system are fit for purpose in the modern age without a carefully constructed land value tax.

The reasons for this have been known to the initiated since Adam Smith. They are too often ignored and indeed kept from the wider public by vested interests. This book is a primer for anyone who wants to help create a more equitable, efficient and sustainable Britain.

There are few people in Britain today who have done more than Tony Vickers to bring the land question back into public debate. In the past decade, numerous studies by and for governments in these islands have come and gone, some of which have acknowledged the beneficial attributes of land value tax (LVT) but all of which gather dust. Some have had too narrow a remit; others have preached to the converted and used language that makes 'real world' politicians and commentators cringe. There is a danger in overstating the case for LVT of which Vickers is aware.

I commend this book to any radical of whatever party who supports a free market system but believes markets are there to serve society and not be their master. As Mark Twain famously said of land: 'They don't make it any more.' That perception – give or take a polder or two – is what makes land both unique and capable of creating such roller coasters of wealth and poverty both within generations and between them. It is up to governments to intervene where markets fail. Without land value taxation, the land market in Britain is bound to fail to deliver the homes and communities we need. If the Government does not soon intervene to recycle Britain's land values, we may not run out of land but we will run out of time to secure a fair, free and sustainable society.

Chris Huhne MP
House of Commons, July 2007

Abstract

THE ISSUE OF 'economic rent' is at the root of poverty, economic justice and sustainability. For modern society to survive and prosper, we need to ensure that the cost of Nature's contribution is charged to beneficiaries and users. That implies a complete shift in the burden of taxation, off enterprise and onto resource usage. Land is the most significant resource: finite and ever more value-laden.

There is now a growing realization across the political spectrum and in relation to several key topical 'doorstep' issues (housing, urban degradation and crime, transport and agriculture) – in Britain and elsewhere – of the need for a Tax Shift. In many fields there have been calls for a land value tax (LVT) but there remains vagueness and confusion as to what such a tax entails and how it would operate. The debate in professional and political classes has been strangely ill-informed, with little understanding of the Law of Rent, of the fundamental nature and scope of LVT as a policy instrument for radical social and economic reform, or of the reasons why other apparently similar taxes are bound to fail.

Drawing on several years of research by the author into the politics and mechanics of property tax reform worldwide, this book sets out why LVT is needed and how it can be implemented in modern Britain over the next two Parliaments (ten years). It includes definitions of Economic Rent and LVT; a short history of land and property taxes; examples of how land rent is captured elsewhere in the world; the drawbacks of other so-called 'land taxes'; the reasons why now is a good time to start implementing LVT in Britain; and some pitfalls and tips on how to manage the transition from taxing 'goods' to taxing 'bads' (i.e. waste rather than work).

The book concludes by departing from *terra firma* to give a taste of some other sources of 'rent as revenue' that constitute Common

Wealth waiting to be recycled. Finally there is a glossary, bibliography and list of websites.

With the centenary of Lloyd George's Peoples Budget approaching, we need to recall Winston Churchill's words then: '*the Land monopoly is the mother of all monopolies*' and also '*Liberalism attacks monopoly*'. Liberals and Liberal Democrats have been singing '*The Land Belongs to the People*' ever since – but the fight to reclaim it needs actions, not words. Baby-boomers emerging into the twenty-first century are the pre-eminent generation of cradle-snatchers: robbing our children and grand-children of their inheritance. This book is to help them take it back from us, as is their right: to 'recycle' Britain's Common Wealth.

Introduction

TAXES ARE NOT just a means of financing government. They are also a vital part of any government's toolkit, instruments for shaping public policy, used primarily to redistribute wealth, although not always as governments intend.

The one source of wealth that no particular member of human society – personal or corporate – creates is what classical economists like Ricardo unfortunately called 'land', to contrast it with 'capital' and 'labour'. This isn't just 'rolling acres', as the word conjures up in modern urban minds. Take away all the products of human-kind and our species itself and you have Land – or rather Nature: that which exists but is not made. It is the activities of society in general, acting on Nature, that create all wealth: discovering, forging, trading, entertaining, communicating, recycling, etc.

Tax any or all of those activities or their products and a government will find that in addition to filling its coffers it will make active sectors of society poorer. Most taxes are (more or less) simple transfers of wealth from private hands into public coffers, from those who create and sustain wealth and quality of life to those who claim either to consume it through public works 'better' than we do or to be able to redistribute it more fairly than can a free market economy.

But those who have taken – or been given title to – mere possession of natural resources also **acquire** wealth, without in any sense creating it. As Winston Churchill put it nearly a century ago, when he was a Liberal:

> *'Roads are made ... services are improved ... and all the while the landlord sits still. Every one of these improvements is effected by the labour and cost of other people and by the*

> *taxpayers. To not one of those improvements does the land monopolist, as a land monopolist, contribute, and yet by every one of them the value of his land is enhanced. He renders no service to the community, he contributes nothing to the general welfare, he contributes nothing to the process from which his own enrichment is derived.'*

Taxes on that kind of wealth cannot make society as a whole poorer, because they do not take away anything that has been 'earned' in the true meaning of the word. Yet such taxes achieve as much, pound for pound, in revenue terms, as any other tax. Moreover every pound taken from those who possess rights to natural resources enables one pound less to be taken from the creative, active members of society, helping to reclaim our Common Wealth for the benefit of society as a whole. Here is the natural fund to pay for all public services and infrastructure.

So when Charles Kennedy, in his first speech to new Liberal Democrat MPs after the 2005 election, said: '*No area of policy will be more crucial over the course of this Parliament than taxation*', he was calling for his Party to lead a debate on how to distribute the tax burden and distribute wealth. Hopefully the words of his Party's mid-term manifesto early in the first New Labour Government still mean something to those who take that debate forward: '*We would ... create a more sustainable and fairer tax system by shifting taxation onto pollution and resource usage and off people ...*'

This book is not about taxes on pollution, which are what most people normally think of as 'environmental' taxes. Instead it deals with 'resource rents as revenue', which is the 'resource usage' part of an environmentally friendly Tax Shift with far greater potential to transform society and economies. It sets out to chart a way of making Britain, over the next ten years or so, a much fairer, more enterprising society, 'liberal' socially **and** economically, whilst crucially helping us to value and conserve natural resources. It is not an economic text-book but is aimed at the general reader who understands, perhaps far better than tax experts and economists, that something is very wrong in the current tax system. When Value Added is the name of a tax, yet ownership of a derelict plot of housing land (or a plot with an empty house on it) almost anywhere in southeast England can 'earn' more for its owner in a year – tax free – than the after-tax income of a typical commuter, something is rotten.

I first outline what is – and what is not – a Land Value Tax (LVT), in the broadest sense, before giving a short history of failed attempts to introduce it in Britain as well as successful instances elsewhere. There is a section on the 'why' of 'rent as revenue' which I hope will stimulate interest in the 'how' that follows. Most of the book then focuses on the present UK context and on land as *terra firma*: LVT as a sub-set of more general 'resource revenues'. My contention is that three things have changed in recent years – information technology, environmentalism and the ending of communism – so that the time is now ripe for LVT to make a major contribution to Tax Shifting. The book deals with a number of what I call 'dead-end' options which might seem attractive in the short term but unlike LVT have no potential to transform modern society. My own preferred policy path is sensitive to political and technical realities. It draws on over six years' research with colleagues at Kingston University and elsewhere and moves debate away from the localized and tired-sounding Site Value Rating towards more economically powerful **national** tax reforms, with local government retaining a share of the cake.

The fascinating thing about the subject of this book to someone who is steeped in liberal politics is that the idea and the policies that flow from it can appeal right across the political spectrum. LVT draws together thoughtful Greens like Jean Lambert, free marketeers like Samuel Brittain, socialists[1] like Dave Wetzel (Vice Chair of Ken Livingstone's Transport for London) and many who swim in the political mainstream in today's centre-left mixed-economy. The book concludes with a flavour of other 'global commons' that can benefit from the magic touch of Tax Shifting with little apparent connection to 'land' as we know it.

Finally I offer copious further reading and web-sites for those who wish to investigate the subject further. I hope this book will stimulate a debate that should dominate Gordon Brown's first years

1 The Labour Representation Committee, which claims nine MPs among its 900 members, recently endorsed LVT.

after wearing Lloyd George's mantle of radical economic reform, as we approach the centenary of The Peoples Budget of 1909.

Our credit-driven society is living on borrowed time. The subject is not just how money transfers between governments and people but is about the economic relationship between humanity and our planet: the only one we've got. It is that important to us all, but most of all to our children from whom we borrow Nature.

What is LVT?

THE PHRASE 'Land Value Taxation' is often used by others to mean something different to what its advocates mean, which is:

> '*... a method of raising public revenue by means of an annual tax on the rental*[2] *value of land. It would replace, not add to, existing taxes.*' (The Land Value Taxation Campaign – LVTC)

Other taxes capture 'land value' – what has been called 'the unearned increment' that inevitably accrues to title holders – but do so in a different way, usually through one-off levies at the time of a transaction or other event involving development, sale, award of planning permission, etc. These are **not** Land Value Taxation but are Land Taxes. LVT is a sub-set of land taxes. Land taxes other than LVT have an entirely different economic effect, although their ethical justification may be the same, i.e. that it is equitable to return

---

2 A distinction should be drawn between pure LVT (in the above definition) and more common but technically impure versions that use capital valuations, not rental value assessments. Most jurisdictions that use LVT assess capital value and then set a very low rate: in North America the rate is expressed as 'mils', i.e. thousandths of the assessed capital value. Although most commercial property transactions are expressed as rental value and business rates in Britain are based on rental – not capital – value, the largest number of taxpayers are homeowners and the housing market operates nowadays primarily on sales not market rents. Hence it is easier and more transparent to base residential LVT, like council tax, on capital values.

However all twentieth century British attempts at LVT/SVR were framed – like the rating system they were to replace – so as to work on rental value, as is shown by the definition of 'site value' used in the 1931 Finance Act:

> *The annual site value of a land unit shall be the annual rent which the land comprising the land unit might be expected to realise if demised with vacant possession at the valuation date in the open market by a willing lessor upon a perpetually renewable tenure upon the assumptions that at that date:*
> *(a) there were not upon or in that land unit:*
> *(i) any buildings erections or works except roads; and*
> *(ii) anything growing except grass heather gorse sedge or other natural growth;*

the unearned increment in land value from the beneficiaries to the community at large that created that value. The reasons why other land taxes are much inferior to LVT – often actually counter-productive economically – will be explained later.

There are three main differences between LVT and other land taxes:

- The **first** is that LVT is based upon a regular assessment of the value of every parcel of land in the jurisdiction levying it, whereas most land taxes are based upon the transaction price of the particular parcel – or a surrogate such as its assessed value – at a specified event. So LVT is an annual tax on value (‘*ad valorem*’), not a one-off tax on price or a surrogate for price.

  In the first sense, that of being *ad valorem* rather than a transaction tax, LVT is like the old rating system or the current British non-domestic rates (NDR). Like them, it needs to have **regular** assessments if the tax base is not to degrade over time and become increasingly inequitable. It is not the rating system or property tax in general that makes it ‘unfair’ but failure to update valuations. It is quite perverse to object to a revaluation for any *ad valorem* tax, because without regular revaluations it is bound to be unfair.[3]

  Most modern taxes, whether LVT or based on ‘gross’ property values like NDR, undergo more frequent revaluations than do the British property taxes. Technology has greatly reduced the cost – both relative to collection costs for other taxes and as a proportion of the revenue such taxes can raise – of carrying out

2 *continued:*

(b) the annual rent had been computed without taking into account the value of any tillages or manures or any improvements for which any sum would by law or custom be payable to an outgoing tenant of a holding;

(c) the land unit were free from any incumbrances except such of the following incumbrances as would be binding upon a purchaser: easements; rights of common; customary rights; public rights; liability to repair highways by reason of tenure; liability to repair the chancel of any church; liability in respect of the repair or maintenance of embankments or sea or river walls; liability to pay any drainage rate under any statute; restrictions upon user which have become operative imposed by or in pursuance of any Act or by any agreement not being a lease.

3 Income tax would be just as unfair if personal incomes were only assessed every five or ten years and during the intervening years taxes were to be based on out-of-date assessments of income.

revaluations. This has been acknowledged by Ministers and by professionals: a past President of the Rating Surveyors Association[4] said in the journal ***Valuer***:

> *'With the advent of modern computer technology and information systems, we have the ability to achieve revaluations on a national scale with a frequency previously unimaginable. We should now be looking seriously at the concept of annual revaluations ...'* (Heard 2005)

Timeliness or up-to-dateness is not the only measure of quality of an *ad valorem* property tax assessment system. Good assessments ought to be carried out by professional valuers, working independently of the tax-setting authority and immune from political interference. In some jurisdictions, tax assessors are either political appointees or work for people who are. Land value can be systematically under-assessed under subtle pressure from politicians who are connected to large landowners, particularly where Computer Aided Mass Assessment (CAMA) and Geographic Information Systems (GIS) are not yet used and assessments rely more on personal subjective judgement. Even where the assessments are required to be split into land and buildings elements, there is a natural tendency for the former to be under-assessed as the latter are over-assessed. Delays in reassessment inevitably lead to this, because buildings deteriorate over time whereas land value increases as prosperity increases, other things being equal. The result is inequity. Good, frequent assessments have significant benefits to a local economy, similar to those described below for 'pure LVT', even when the property tax on building values is set at the same rate as on land values.

LVT purists would have a uniform rate of tax applied to all classes of land, according to what is known as its highest and best use (HABU) within the legal limits set by planning or zoning laws. In order to fairly and accurately assess land value, tax assessors need to know what is/are the permissible use(s) to which a

4 Jon Heard IRRV was 2004 President of RSA and is a consultant to Underwoods Chartered Surveyors.

parcel of land can be put. They then discount the actual use and the actual buildings on each site, just as a developer would when appraising a site for redevelopment. To then also moderate the tax rate for special classes of use, such as housing or farming, would be to account twice for the difference in HABU value that flows from a new planning permission or zoning ordinance. Unfortunately, special pleading by powerful interest groups and voters again puts pressure on governments to grant exemptions and discounted tax rates to certain classes of land use or owner.

- The **second** difference is that 'land' means the site alone, excluding any 'improvements' to it, such as buildings, crops, drainage or other works done to it that have enhanced its value. With LVT it is ...

  '*... assumed that all neighbouring properties are developed as at the time of the valuation; other things being equal, a vacant site in a row of houses would therefore be assessed at the same value as the adjacent sites occupied by houses.*'
  (LVTC)

  'Land' in English law is synonymous with 'landed property' and 'real estate'. Hence land taxes are synonymous with property taxes, as in Stamp Duty Land Tax – which is certainly **not** LVT. Property seldom transfers in an unimproved state, so that the valuation of land alone requires specialized techniques. These are covered later.

- A **third** distinction made between LVT and most other land and property taxes is that it is levied on the owner not the occupier. The complex nature of British land ownership is often cited as a reason why it cannot be introduced here. The more likely reason is the absence of a land register[5] that defines who owns title and benefits from the rental value of land.

5 Her Majesty's Land Registry (HMLR) aims to achieve a 'Comprehensive Register' for England and Wales by about 2015 and is resourced for this. However a decision to adopt LVT would provide a 'trigger' for completing the Register, for which only secondary legislation is needed.

Why is it Such a Good Idea?

THE LVTC LEAFLET *What is Land Value Taxation?* sets out a number of 'advantages' that follow from LVT. These can be matched against the 'aspects of tax policy' in the document setting out the remit of the Liberal Democrat Tax 'Commission' (Policy Working Group), which included recommendations for LVT in its report to the party conference in 2006 (Liberal Democrat Party 2006).

Contemporary features of modern Britain reinforce these aspects in five 'dimensions': politics, economics, tax administration, culture and ethics. Both the *pros* and the *cons* of the tax are highlighted in each dimension.

Politically, 'Pandora's Box' cannot be shut now that the mould of British politics appears to have been broken by the creation of devolved administrations. In Scotland, Wales and London, we now have what London's Transport Commissioner Bob Kiley – upturning his native America's cry for independence – called 'Representation without Taxation'. To create a geographically defined government without adequate means of raising funds to pay for the things it is empowered to do is to create conditions in which a campaign for new tax-raising powers is inevitable. A tax that defines itself by the same boundaries of land that are used for government has natural appeal to leaders of devolved administrations. All who own land in Scotland, whether Scottish or not, benefit or suffer from what the Scottish Government does with its money. With all other taxes claimed already by Whitehall/Westminster, LVT and reform of property taxes become appealing.

> On the negative side, despite steady growth in support for the Lib Dems and minor parties, the Westminster electoral system makes it unlikely that **any** radical tax reform will be initiated by a one-party UK Government. That system makes a

Aspects[6] of Tax Policy considered by Lib Dem Tax Commission

Aspect	LVTC claimed advantage	Remarks
Simplicity	*'LESS BUREAUCRACY'... straightforward, once the system has settled down.'*	Not self-evident. However several recent studies of property taxes (e.g. in Germany and South Africa) have concluded that LVT would be cheaper and simpler than current property tax.
Efficiency	*'A MORE EFFICIENT LAND MARKET'*; also *'if we tax labour, buildings or machinery and plant, we discourage people from constructive and beneficial activities and penalize enterprise and efficiency.'*	a Occupation of land matches its location with more appropriate activities; b By enabling other taxes to be reduced, productivity increases and 'deadweight' costs also reduce; c Cost of collection and compliance is low, after initial introduction.
Fairness	*'Land value owes nothing to individual effort and everything to the competing needs of the community ... Conversely, the reward for individual effort can belong only to the one who earns it.'*	LVT is equitable and accords with economic justice. 'Fairness' is not the same as 'ability to pay'. If individuals can acquire spending power through unearned wealth in the value of land under their homes, surely it is fair to require them to relinquish some of that wealth through tax? Arguably it is more fair than taxing their earned income.
(Competitiveness)	*'MARGINAL AREAS REVITALISED ... creates tax havens where they are needed ... competition makes it impossible [under LVT] for a business producing goods on a valuable site to charge more than one producing similar goods on less valuable land ... will stimulate new business and new employment, reducing the need for costly welfare.'*	Supported by early exponents of free market economics, LVT is seen as a precondition of Free Trade and competition, partly by encouraging efficient use of land and partly by allowing other taxes to be alleviated. The countries that use LVT, such as Hong Kong, tend to exemplify both free enterprise and prosperity. Britain would gain competitive advantage by adopting it early, while breaking no trade rules.

6 In the published policy paper ***Fairer, Simpler, Greener***, several of these 'aspects' (which became 'key principles') were omitted. They are in brackets in the table.

Aspect	LVTC claimed advantage	Remarks
(Tax avoidance and evasion)	*'NO AVOIDANCE OR EVASION. Land cannot be hidden, removed to a tax haven or concealed in an electronic data system.'*	Unlike most taxes, compliance costs reduce as LVT rate increases. Payment is at worst delayed: owners can reside outside the tax jurisdiction, even if their property is immovable (tax owed is a negative asset).
Sustainability	*'LESS URBAN SPRAWL. Dilapidated inner-city areas are returned to good use, reducing the pressure for building on green-field sites.'*	LVT is supported by most environmental economists because of its positive impact on the conservation of finite resources.
EU Framework	Not covered by LVTC.	LVT could replace VAT as the main source of EU revenue. It would require a standard land valuation system. The International Valuation Standards Committee (IVSC) has already started a process that could enable this, currently affecting only investment property owned by international companies.
Decentralisation to nations, regions and localities	*'AN ESTABLISHED AND PROVEN SYSTEM.'* Most advocates would prefer LVT to be used at national level but accept that it is perfectly acceptable at 'lower' tiers as well.	The principle of 'precepting' of property taxes is well understood and fits well with devolved government: whoever decides spending should be allowed to raise revenue from land values to pay for it. This would overcome what has been called 'the dependency culture' of local government.
(Honesty)	Not covered by LVTC.	Hypothecation, openness and choice are associated with 'honesty'. 'Landvaluescape' exposes the effect of human activity on land values, makes possible hypothecation: cause and effect. Choice is exercised by individuals deciding on locations for economic activity according to LVT rates, not distortions caused by other taxes and subsidies.

Government pay a heavy price for mistakes, as the Canadian Conservatives discovered: defeat can easily become annihilation. At UK level, a fairer voting system (as in existing devolved assemblies and parliaments) that makes consensus on potentially risky radical policies easier to achieve is still some way off. Major parties who are potential coalition partners should ideally share a common objective on LVT. A greater awareness of the policy concept needs first to exist within those parties and among the wider public.

Economics favours taxes that do not hit the economically active or wealth-creating activities. There is a clear gap opening up between what Government knows it needs to spend on infrastructure for a sustainable future and what it can raise from existing taxes. Treasury officials know full well that land values rise when infrastructure is created, also that house prices can be stabilized by LVT. Almost all the economic arguments are in favour of LVT.

However some economists who accept that LVT could plug this funding **gap** seem unable to accept that a tax **shift** could further improve the British economy. Neo-liberal economists would have us believe that a consumer-led economy, based on credit largely backed by personal wealth in land/houses, is the basis for Britain's future. Specifically there is little stomach for dealing with the demand side of the housing market, other than by fuelling it further through easing purchases from a stagnant stock. LVT may be seen as a revenue source but it still isn't seen as a tool for economic regeneration, transformation and efficiency by many.

Tax administrators who take a dispassionate look at property tax systems generally admit that modern methods, which produce site values as a by-product, could reduce their running costs. Using computer aided mass appraisal (CAMA) and geographic information systems (GIS), studies in countries as different as the USA, Germany, South Africa, Lithuania, Mexico and China, have shown this to be the case. Some tax authorities, such as Lucas County, Ohio, and Victoria Australia have led the way towards annual revaluations and the use of regular 'landvaluescape' monitoring and modeling by spatial planners and other public officials to aid decision making. Land value – although not always itself separately taxed – when measured by tax officials supports better governance. Costs of such systems are falling.

However, there is still a significant one-off cost in re-tooling for modern property taxes. Senior tax administrators are not easily persuaded of the non-tax wider benefits and other officials are unaware of how tax reform might benefit them. Value mapping would both enable and benefit from LVT but it requires determination for the case even to be heard that either LVT or value mapping are worth the trouble in transition.

There is also a belief that the complex nature of commercial property ownership in Britain would lead to problems in apportioning the tax among beneficial owners (see box[7] on page 16) and in collecting tax other than via occupiers. This is largely because of the lack of a complete land registry but also connected to the opaqueness of the property market and the extent of foreign corporate offshore ownership of certain classes of property.

The **culture** of deference towards politicians and bureaucrats may be breaking up and a willingness is growing among single-issue campaigners to work together outside conventional politics and put the case for radical reforms direct to the public. There are many such causes that now count LVT as one of their key tools, which was certainly not the case twenty years ago.

Once again however, it is hard to package LVT as a measure that people will take to the streets to achieve. The frustration with existing British local taxes was captured by 'Axe-The-Tax' campaigners, who were seldom also supporters of LVT. In the 1960s and again when the Poll Tax was introduced it was young campaigners that took to the streets in protest: in the current climate the growing 'grey power' lobby naturally abhors wealth

7 Taken from Connellan (2004): Annexe 4 to Ch.10, pp.128-9.

Apportioning LVT to Hierarchical Owners

Assume a property with a typical hierarchical ownership: freeholder, ground lessee, intermediate leaseholder and tenant, such that:

- Freeholder grants 99-year lease to Ground Lessee at rent of £200 p.a.
- Ground Lessee grants a 42-year lease to Lessee at rent of £1,000 p.a.
- Lessee lets to tenant on an occupational tenancy for 20 years at rent of £5,000 p.a.

Freehold owner is the only party assessed to pay LVT, set at x% of annual site value. However, if the owner is not known to the tax authorities, the bill may be served on any of the above parties. They can deduct from the rent they pay to their immediate landlord:

- x% of the assessed annual site value *or*
- x% of the rent that they pay to their landlord

whichever is *less*. This is the **Rule for Apportionment**.

Assume land value is assessed at £1,500 and the LVT rate is 50%, so that the total liability for the property is £750. The bill goes to the occupying tenant, because the other parties are not known to the billing authority (the land being unregistered). Applying the Rule:

- Occupying tenant pays whole LVT bill of £750 and immediately deducts it from payment of rent to Lessee. Tenant pays £5,000 minus £750 = £4,250 to Lessee.
- Lessee, receiving reduced rent of £4,250 from Tenant, can only deduct £500 (50% x £1,000) from rent payment to Ground Lessee, so pays £500.
- Ground Lessee, receiving reduced rent of £500 from Lessee, can only deduct £100 (50% x £200) from rent payable to Freeholder, so pays £100.
- Freeholder receives reduced rent of £100.

The effect is that all parties have been taxed the 'profit rent' that can be ascribed to the land value of the site, which has been distributed among them according to their share of that profit rent. The table summarises this.

Party	Profit Rent Before LVT			Profit Rent After LVT			Reduced Profit Rent = LVT
	Rent Received	Rent Paid	Profit Rent	Rent Received	Rent Paid	Profit Rent	
Tenant[8]	£5,000	£5,000	£0	£4,250	£4,250	£0	£0
Lessee	£5,000	£1,000	£4,000	£4,250	£500	£3,750	£250
Ground Lessee	£1,000	£200	£800	£500	£100	£400	£400
Freeholder	£200	£0	£200	£100	£0	£100	£100
Totals			**£5,000**			**£4,250**	**£750**

8 By definition, tenants receive no net rent – with or without LVT.

> taxes like LVT. Can the anti-establishment protest again capture young peoples' imagination? After all, it is their earned income that alternative tax reforms – like Flat Tax or Local Income Tax – will steal.

Fundamentally, **ethics** should lead us to LVT. What sort of society allows those who capture wealth without lifting a finger to escape taxation, while those who contribute to wealth creation pay taxes out of their earnings and trade? The instinct to find ways around paying taxes on income and capital and feel no guilt is founded in an innate sense that we should 'keep what we make' and 'pay for what we take'.[9] We pay these dysfunctional taxes without too much protest because we want public services to be properly funded. We accept income tax, corporation tax, VAT, capital gains tax, inheritance tax, etc. not because we **like** seeing so much of our hard-earned income taken away but because most of us know of no fairer way to pay for the essential services that government delivers. Resource rents give a gigantic 'free lunch' to those who siphon away our Common Wealth. LVT allows earned income and capital to be retained in greater measure by their rightful owners.

> Unfortunately we are all land monopolists now. In a home-owning democracy, there is a very large – and largely voting – interest group that benefits from a system that gives them spending power without effort. The main sufferers are the disengaged, young, non-voting minority who do not own their own homes and probably never will. They are major consumers of tax expenditure, through public transport, social services, subsidized housing and income support. At an international level, they are the aid recipients and the victims of wars over natural resources like oil reserves. 'Life's a Lottery' is all too true and the fundamental inequity of a system that rewards inactivity and penalizes work and enterprise is kept from society. At every level, the hopelessness that comes with realization that 'common wealth' has been appropriated as permanent 'free lunch' for others feeds the urge to commit crime and

9 Accredited to American Green campaigner Alanna Hartzok (www.earthrights.net).

> terrorist atrocities. However the same hopelessness keeps the victims of the system away from the ballot box.

The time is ripe for LVT in Britain because many of its advantages address topical concerns of voters and administrators. LVT has been raised in conferences on affordable housing, transport funding, climate change, third world poverty and fair trade. Experts in these fields expound on its benefits seriously, thereby acquiring new and influential supporters among those who until recently had never heard of it. Increasingly it is unnecessary to explain what it is or how it can address these issues. Rather the focus of debate is on how to do it within the current political structures and the details of valuation and tax collection. But time and again these new adherents wonder why, if it so good a policy, it hasn't already been implemented.

To understand the answer to that, it is necessary to provide a brief history of the idea and attempts to turn it into reality.

Background History

THE ROOTS OF LVT lie in prehistory. Probably ever since the first settled agrarian societies, it has been understood that all wealth comes from the land through the application of human effort and some help from 'the gods'. The Jubilee of the Old Testament (Leviticus, Ch.25) was not just about debt cancellation. It was seen as important for the natural advantages accruing to those citizens who held rich land to be periodically restored to the community, by re-allocation of land at the time of a Jubilee. Resource rent equalisation went with debt and land transfer cancellation, so that those who 'privatised' natural advantage should restore it to the community. If rulers wanted to raise revenue, they had to tap into that stream of wealth known as economic rent.[10] Michael Hudson,[11] writing in Andelson (2000), notes that alongside dependence on stores of wealth raised in revenue by forms of rent[12] or tithe, governments became creditors rather than the debtors that modern states now are. Hence the link between tax and money systems, which exists today – both modern systems being somewhat dysfunctional.

Revenue for governments from resource rents remained the norm until well into the modern era. Adam Smith well understood the importance of location in economics and the distinction between rent from 'ground' value and from building value, is treated

10 'Economic rent' is, at its simplest, the surplus income that accrues to a person controlling land or other natural resource, beyond that which is necessarily earned by labour and capital applied to it. 'Land' is essentially passive and only beneficial to human society when the other two 'active' factors combine to create wealth. In assigning land rights to persons, society allows economic rent to be privatized – unless those persons are required to pay for those rights, either in 'capitalised rent' by one-off transaction price, or by an annual charge based on the rental value of those rights in the market.

11 Hudson has been President of the Institute for the Study of Long Term Economic Trends (ISLET) since 1996.

12 Rent is here used to mean the actual transfer of a portion of the yield, from land, as opposed to the theoretical concept of economic rent defined earlier.

at length in his Wealth of Nations. He considered that what we call LVT was one of the most appropriate forms of revenue for the state:

> *'Ground-rents and the ordinary rent of land are, therefore, perhaps, the species of revenue which can best bear to have a peculiar tax imposed upon them.'*
>
> (Smith 1776, Bk.5, Ch.2, Pt.2, Art.1)

Few would have argued with him at the time, yet few today who hail Smith as a founder of modern economics would know of his 'land tax tendency'.

For most of the middle ages, monarchs assigned responsibility for raising revenue through the feudal system of land tenure. They gave land rights away to courtiers in exchange for their loyalty in battle, as the need arose to share the rent and revenue that these rights brought. As government revenue needs grew, the tendency to privatize rent also grew, the personal debts of monarchs became permanent and much of the tax revenue went to paying interest on loans. A multiplicity of taxes arose and their burden shifted onto trade and then profits and income.

Meanwhile the right to create money shifted from the State to banks, eventually becoming to all appearances de-coupled from economic rent by not even having to be backed by 'real' wealth in the form of deposits of gold. Today at least 95% of money in circulation is created by banks as credit. But most of that credit is backed by equity in the form of landed property (Rowbotham 2002). The link between the boom/slump cycles in modern economies and property/land values is ably described by Harrison (2005), who is not alone in prescribing LVT as the answer.

David Ricardo, an Englishman writing in 1817 soon after income tax was introduced, was one of the first economists to give land rent, as revenue, a special place in restoring coherence to political economic theory and government. Throughout the nineteenth century, the Land Question was well understood and linked to political reforms that Liberals and then Socialists backed. As European powers colonized the rest of the world, many of them introduced systems of land tenure and taxation that retained most of the rental value from natural resources for their colonial governments to use

– notably not for the natives however. Examples were New Zealand, Chile and Hong Kong, all of which had forms of LVT before Henry George wrote his seminal work 'Progress and Poverty' in 1879.[13]

George's writings and oratory had an enormous impact on politics worldwide between 1880 and 1920, although landed interests were not slow to react. Even before his death in 1897, George – who had no formal education in the subjects upon which he wrote and spoke so eloquently in every continent – had managed to energise most of the academic, religious and commercial establishment against his ideas. Yet Australia, South Africa, Denmark, Russia, China, Japan, Britain and Ireland all either had LVT on the statute book or were in the process of introducing it when the first World War broke out. Communism eclipsed what was beginning to be known as 'Georgism' but was in fact a key component of Liberalism.

The reforming British Liberal government of one hundred years ago led the way in tackling 'The Land Question' through LVT, until their Lordships blocked Lloyd George's Peoples Budget of 1909. The fervour of its supporters then is hard to imagine now. Anticipating opposition from landowners – some within his own party – Lloyd George had watered down his proposals even before his Finance Act was defeated by the Tory majority in the Lords. This triggered the Parliament Act that to this day prevents 'money bills' being interfered with by the unelected Upper House. Nevertheless it is true to say that the Welfare State as we know it was to have been largely funded from what the then Prime Minister Campbell-Bannerman, had promised *'to make ... less of a pleasure-ground for the rich and more of a treasure-house for the nation ...'*: the land (Gaffney 1998). Revenue from LVT would have been divided equally between central and local government.

From both left and right of the political spectrum a kind of conspiracy arose to expunge from curricula the idea that 'land' was a distinct factor in economics from 'capital' (Gaffney & Harrison 1994). Economic theories grew up that ignored geography and the finite limits of the world and its resources. Meanwhile those

13 Between its publication and his death in 1897, George's *Progress and Poverty* outsold Marx's *Das Capital* and it remains the most widely read book on political economy of all time. By 1902, the Bible was the only book of any kind more widely read (Braund 2005).

examples of 'value capture' that survived generally flourished, sometimes spread but often mutated and were disfigured by complications and compromises. In Russia and China, social liberals who understood and promoted LVT, like Sun Yat-Sen, Kerensky and Tolstoy, fled, died or were overtaken by idealogues of the Left. But vestiges of LVT – or at least the memory – remained in Taiwan, Korea, the Baltic States and much of Eastern Europe. Ironically its progress in some parts of the world during the mid-twentieth century was due to British colonial administrators who had seen it working elsewhere in the Empire.

In 1931, a Labour Government enacted LVT as a national tax but then succumbed to division under the National Government, whose Tory majority repealed the measure before it could be implemented. Every Labour Government attempt since then to capture land values for revenue has used one-off transfer taxes and not LVT.[14] The notion that 'God Gave the Land to the People' survived not just in song at Liberal conferences but through the United Committee for the Taxation of Land Values, formed in 1929 from hundreds of local campaign groups set up before World War One. This venerable but increasingly obscure body changed its name twice later in the twentieth century and is now a charity named after Henry George.

Although the Liberal Party was faithful to LVT until the merger with the SDP (the 'continuing Liberal Party' still is), most of those who joined it after about 1960 had little or no knowledge of the policy and had never been taught classical land economics at school or university. In Britain it was regarded as an anachronism, belonging to an age when 'land' was associated with the horse-drawn plough. Whereas the support for LVT fell in line with the fall in electoral support for the Liberals between 1920 and 1960, it did not rise as the Liberals recovered. In fact it lived on through the twentieth century perhaps as much in the Labour Party which, after disposing of its State Socialist baggage during the Thatcher Government, was still home to significant numbers of politicians who had been taught about Henry George by their parents. LVT is a core idea of

---

14 As recently as 1946 LVT could attract over 150 signatures of Labour MPs for an Early Day Motion in Parliament. Herbert Morrison had presented the London Rating (Site Values) Bill to Parliament in 1939 and attracted 135 votes.

Britain's centre-left, a red-and-gold thread running through the tangled century of collectivism and monetarism.

A late twentieth century strand of political thought, scarcely existing at the time of Henry (or Lloyd) George, was crucial to giving new life to LVT: environmentalism. It has been said that if George was alive today he would be in the Green Party. Certainly many 'greens' have taken to him, perhaps not knowing that he also espoused Free Trade. It has been Greens in Canada, Scotland and Australia that have recently made most of the running with the policy.

Since about 1970, the anti-sprawl movement and those calling for 'sustainable urban renewal' have taken increasing interest in LVT, more as a means of incentivising appropriate development than as a revenue raising mechanism. The split-rate tax in Pennsylvania was used primarily to rejuvenate cities not treasuries, although it was understood to have that effect as well. Lord Rogers, in his 1999 report for John Prescott's Urban Task Force, drew attention to the experience of these cities. It has been as a measure to finance particular urban and transport projects rather than as a major source of general revenues that LVT has been looked at in recent years. Unquestionably public investment in such projects is 'recycled' as land value uplift. However it is beginning to be realized that separating the effect of any one cause of land value change from the effects of others is extremely difficult. Attempting to finance just one project (e.g. CrossRail in London) from a hypothecated land value fund introduces either inequities or complexities – or both. So the policy wheel may now be coming full circle, with LVT once again a candidate for replacing general taxes at one or more levels of government.

In November 2006, the world body for tackling urban poverty UN-HABITAT, declared LVT to be '*in accord with Millennium Development Goal 7*', which includes '*integrate the principles of sustainable development into country policies and programmes; reverse loss of environmental resources.*' They placed a contract with Earth Rights Institute, a network of some 30 LVT experts worldwide, coordinated by American Green activist Alanna Hartzok, to develop a program on land value capture and taxation as a 'global land tool' for governments, to be completed by August 2007. The contract (UN-HABITAT 2006) states, for background:

'The natural world is rightfully the common property of all persons, and therefore the LVT is not really a tax, but simply the collection of rent (a user fee) on behalf of the community. For eight thousand years worldwide, LVT has been the primary basis for producing public revenue and is easy for people to understand. LVT is the appropriate instrument for the urgent fight against global inequity and poverty.'

LVT Around the World Today

THE FOLLOWING examples are just a few of those described in a recent book on the subject, in which the American editor summarises the recent history of LVT:

> *The implementation of LVT has really been extremely modest, and its impact, where genuine, all too often blunted by countervailing policies, usually at other levels of government ... Wherever [it] has a foothold, it is essential that the officials charged with its administration be educated as to its advantages, both technical and moral, that this education be ongoing, and, insofar as possible, extended to the general population.* (Andelson 2000)

Despite their modest nature, all the implementations described below have been incontestably successful policy measures. If LVT has been in retreat worldwide, it is not because it has since failed but because it has never been pursued with sufficient determination and its wider economic benefits have not been made clear enough to the public when the inevitable vested interests made their attack on it.

Major global economies of the modern world – Japan, Taiwan, Hong Kong – arguably owe much of their late twentieth-century economic transformation to LVT. Yet, as Andelson's contributors describe, in all three the policy has either disappeared or is in disrepute, neglect and/or under attack. Yet Russia and China both show signs of wishing to use LVT to help make massive economic and social progress in the near future, to the extent that the rest of the world may need to respond in like manner. The examples given here are not of past failures or future prospects but of what is actually happening now by way of land value capture for public revenue.

Hong Kong

From the time it was first colonized by the British, all land except that assigned to the Anglican cathedral was retained by the Crown as a deliberate policy of retaining control over development of the economy. Consequently a large proportion of revenue has always accrued to the government from lease sales and ground rents. Typically in the 1990s this amounted to about forty percent of revenue, although it fluctuates with the economic cycle. Developers are reluctant to pay Land Premium when the market is falling.[15]

Hong Kong does not operate LVT. However it combines a vigorous capitalist economy with by far the largest recovery of Common Wealth in land values as revenue, because the success of the economy expressed in high land value accrues largely to government and not to private land-holders. At every renewal of leasehold contract, modification of lease conditions or transfer of lease, Government as freeholder revalues sites and negotiates increased payments as part of its urban renewal strategy.[16] Urban extensions are carried out by annual auctions of state-owned sites, thus preventing much of the speculation which occurs in countries like the UK where private land ownership is allowed. In this way, planning restrictions can be imposed much more fairly and transparently. The tax is known as Land Premium.

There are however problems with this system. The huge sums involved in Land Premium leasehold sales mean that small developers are virtually excluded from the land market and a cartel operates to the disadvantage of Government. Also, in contrast to the way LVT captures land value, the Government is unable to capture 'spill-over' land value uplift on sites already developed that results from new development nearby, until many years later when leases come up for renewal.

For these reasons, many in Hong Hong wish to modify the Land Premium system by 'annualising' payments: agreeing in the initial sale contract to re-assess land values periodically and to convert the

15 The City of London Corporation also benefits significantly from being a major landowner – not just of land in the City but even beyond Greater London. Capitalism can thrive without private freehold ownership of property.

16 China's 2007 Property Act similarly retains freehold land ownership for the state and taxes leaseholders when they sell their leases.

huge up-front payments into annual stages which would improve the cash-flow of payees and government – and be fairer.

Land Premium and other property taxes finance more than three-quarters of all Hong Kong's capital expenditure. This fulfils the role of 'planning gain' in a more transparent way than where, as in UK, land is in freehold private ownership. This is the main reason that taxes on income and profits are so low by international standards for developed countries, whilst public services approach the highest quality.

Australia

By far the most advanced application of LVT in the world, in terms of closeness to the ideal as well as proportion of total revenues, is Australia. In some respects, all three tiers of government (Federal 'Commonwealth', state and local) use LVT. At Federal level, land value revenue is collected through leasehold rental payments on Commonwealth owned land: LVT on other land was also collected by the Commonwealth between 1912 and 1952. Across all tiers, LVT and other forms of land rent collected currently amount to 8.6% of Australia's taxes in 2005/6 (about A$1,250 per person per year).

LVT is universal in Queensland and New South Wales as the local tax and predominant in Western Australia. It is also used by all state governments, yielding on average *per capita* between A$45 and A$100 per year, or some A$1200m in revenue. There are wide variations in the incidence of the tax, as regards exemptions and percentage rates for specific land use categories, which leads to perverse anomalies such as that which has led environmentalists to oppose LVT in NSW. Here the farmers obtained exemption from LVT for land under cultivation or 'improved' grazing, thereby giving an incentive to take conservation land under the plough or otherwise destroy native biodiversity. Of course this is not the fault of LVT *per se* but of the way in which 'special pleading' has corrupted the idea. Many other categories of land use in NSW are given lower rates of tax or full exemption, which puts more pressure on land taxed at the full rate and increases general resistance to the tax. It should never be necessary to introduce differential rates, because the true assessed value should already take account of the 'ability to pay' of every site.

Australia has some of the most advanced methods of assessment of site value in the world. Recently both the Victoria and Queensland state governments modernized their valuation systems and made the basis of the tax more transparent to politicians and the public. Nevertheless there are indications that a general shift in the 'wrong' direction is occurring, possibly because home-owners are a powerful lobby group and prefer to see income and expenditure taxed than their wealth. Another reason for the fall in LVT yield is a decline in Australian land values during the early 1990s.

New Zealand

New Zealand has had LVT since it was colonized by the British. SVR was easily the largest source of revenue for local government until the late 1980s, having been introduced voluntarily by local plebiscite into about three quarters of municipalities during the twentieth century and hardly ever abandoned by any local council. This indicates how popular and successful it proved to local voters.

However the country's economic crisis of the 1970s and political reforms in the 1980s – specifically a reorganization of local government into far fewer larger authorities – led to the adoption by some of the new councils of one of three other forms of property tax allowed. The right of local voters to call for reversion to SVR by plebiscite was removed. Since property tax reform is such a sensitive issue for a political party to campaign on at local elections, SVR has been slow to return to its former predominance. Nevertheless it remains the most common form of local tax in New Zealand, with two thirds of local authorities using a land value basis only. The overall proportion of local revenues secured from site values has however fallen from 80% to 40% since 1984, because it has tended to be the larger cities that abandoned SVR.

Denmark

Until the accession of ten new countries in 2004, Denmark was the only EU country with LVT. Its successful use of the tax has often been cited in British studies, most recently in the Barker Report on housing supply. It has had the tax since the 1920s, as a source of revenue for local government securing about 7% of budget needs. For a brief period in the 1950s Denmark had a coalition Ground

Duty Government that was pledged '*to increase LVT as much as possible*'.

In 2005, local government reorganization was combined with property tax modernization. The local tax offices have been taken over by the central tax authority SKAT. In the new single-tier local authorities, LVT can be set at between 2.6% and 4%. In addition, there has since 2000 been a tax like business rate levied on owner-occupied **domestic** property alone and administered through the income tax system. There is a separate tax on most commercial property. Although centrally administered, all these taxes go to pay for local government.

The Danish property tax system is extremely efficient and transparent, with revaluations every other year based on all transactions in the previous four years.[17] Nevertheless administration costs are far lower than in Britain (about £1.50 per property per year, compared to £6 in UK). All the different property taxes use a single central property database, which links a gazetteer covering all land parcels and buildings in the country to highly detailed maps and details of the use and ownership of property and to electoral registers. Telephone directories used to carry the site values of properties alongside the phone numbers of their owners. It is made quite transparent to homeowners how their site value is calculated and soon they will have online access to maps showing valuations nation-wide. There is a very low level of appeals against site value assessments, however this may be partly because the tax rate is low.

Tax policy officials in the finance ministry would like to increase the yield of LVT although there have been a few High Court cases recently where owners have successfully appealed against land-only tax assessments, on the basis that there are too few bare land sales in urban areas to provide comparison. This has led some to suggest that LVT is contrary to human rights and indefensible in law, so that despite the lack of serious political opposition to LVT and the existence of the most modern technical systems, it might founder.

17 Both Denmark and Sweden were visited by the author in late 2005, to discover the status of their property tax systems. Reports are at www.landvaluescape.org/archives/000074.html.

Of particular interest to those who support moves to use LVT to finance transport investment in Britain is the method adopted for financing Copenhagen's first mass transit system. The entire LVT yield from land being redeveloped in a large area of dockland, which is being linked by the metro to the city centre, has been hypothecated to the joint venture company formed by the two cities affected and their developer partner. The development body has raised a Bond using the collateral of the expected LVT income stream. Ironically the idea for this came, it is said, from a visit to London's Docklands in the 1980s, when the GLC was proposing something similar which the UK Government blocked.

Baltic States

All three new Baltic States (Latvia, Lithuania and Estonia) exhibited strong interest in LVT as soon as Soviet rule ended. With ethnic links to Scandinavia, they naturally leaned towards the Scandinavian model for economic and social reforms post-communism. They also had a pre-Communist memory of the ideas of Henry George and a well educated administrative and professional class. Their modern land reforms seek to re-establish a strong property market and wide home ownership. Their monetary and fiscal policies share a desire to remain competitive within the EU, stabilize prices and make adequate resources available to local governments.

Given the above, it was not surprising that all three countries turned to Denmark and other sources of expertise in LVT to help establish modern cadastral land information and tax systems. They have developed flexible but different systems and liaise closely with each other and with neighbouring transitional states.

Estonia introduced LVT as early as 1993, for both the small number of private land owners and for occupiers of state land prior to privatization, with all the revenue since 1996 going to municipalities. Tax rate is within limits 0.1% to 2.5%, decided annually by councils. The National Land Board undertakes regular mass revaluations (1996 and 2001) and tax collection is also undertaken by the state for councils. As the national cadastre neared completion in 1999, discussion of LVT as a source of national revenue began. The land tax only accounts for about one percent of all revenue, although in some rural local authorities it yields nearly one third of their budget requirement. It is widely acknowledged to have assisted a smooth transition to property ownership while discouraging speculative land holding.

Lithuania's land tax does not extend to homeowners but its property tax administrators expect it to do so before long. Until 2006 the tax was based on non-market, crude assessments, while modern systems were installed. The land information and valuation systems are now advanced, transparent, market based, regularly updated and comprehensive, financed by levies on purchasers of state land. From 2006 these assessments largely replaced those used initially.[18] Despite a very fast-growing economy, there is extensive under-use of land and LVT is seen as an incentive tax that ensures appropriate development and discourages speculation. The only political party to explicitly favour LVT in the 2004 elections was the Conservative Party, apparently seeing it as the best way to keep taxes on enterprise low and speed up land privatization. However there is, according to officials in the National Land Service, a widespread understanding among politicians that LVT is an effective policy. There is no real problem with the technical matter of separating land value from gross property value, because the property market is so active and the systems used for assessment are so modern.

Latvia completed its basic land cadastre before the other two countries but has been slower to adopt modern property tax assessment systems. Its land tax is somewhat cruder but it seems to be moving towards LVT at a similar level of yield and for similar reasons. Tax assessments are only tenuously based on market transactions for rural land but have used transaction data from the Land Register in urban areas since 2000. However from 2006 a new law requires all valuations to be market-based and also simultaneous 4-yearly nation-wide tax revaluations for each class of real property. Latvia has a substantial property transfer tax, which has led to problems with participants colluding to artificially depress prices to avoid tax. The growth of a mortgage industry should help end this.

18 Although a new buildings tax, introduced in 2006, is based on market value, the land tax remains for the time being based on nominal values and not derived from CAMA. However 'in nearest future Parliament is going to analyze the issue on basing land tax on market value' (Aleksiene and Bagnadovicius 2006).

United States

Land hunger was what drew people to America voluntarily and Americans naturally associate land with economic opportunity. For most of its history, the USA relied heavily on taxation of land values at state and local level but with the changed teaching of economic theory that followed George's demise (Gaffney & Harrison 1994) the industrial revolution led Americans to dissociate land wealth from tax revenue. Also other Federal sources of revenue and spending programmes swamped the traditional local ones.

Henry George appeared on the scene at a turbulent time. His ideals did not impress most of the American establishment, which confidently expected free market capitalism to be able to deal with all the ills that were already becoming obvious in the transition to an industrial economy. A few 'single tax' communities carried forward those ideals but gradually shrunk to insignificance. LVT principles were adopted elsewhere for specific infrastructure projects (irrigation, mass transit) and the separation of land and building values in property tax assessment was enshrined in law in most states early on, which provided a sound basis for modern reforms that focus on abatement of the buildings or 'improvements' element. Crucially, property tax payment remains invariably the responsibility of property owners and not occupiers.

Local autonomy has been crucial to the advance of property tax reform in the US and revival of interest in LVT. Simply by having an honest and thorough reassessment of split values, with realistic land value assessments backed by powers to acquire at owners' valuation, many cities have in effect seen land value capture reinvigorate their economies. However the most impressive evidence in support of LVT has been provided by the twenty or so 'two-rate tax' cities in Pennsylvania (PA).

There are two main ways in which split valuations have been used in PA. Firstly state-wide, owners who invest in new commercial properties can have up to 100% of the value of those structures exempt from the state's property tax, reducing this exemption on a sliding scale over up to ten years. There is no exemption from the land value element of the property tax under these laws.

Secondly and more important to ordinary voters, cities can choose to adopt 'split-rate' for their municipal property tax, on all categories of property. The state requires the transition to split-rate to be revenue neutral over five years,[19] during which period the rate on land value rises and that on building value falls. The differential in some cities has reached as high as 12:1 but is usually around 3:1. Because property taxes are not paid in respect of land owned by public or charitable bodies[20] and are also paid to overlapping county and school board jurisdictions which cannot adopt split-rate, the impact is quite limited. Nevertheless even a small shift towards land values has been shown to have a significant effect (see below, under Regeneration).

In the case of Allentown, an industrial city of 100,000 people west of New York, the city charter now has a clause that says all new tax levies will be financed solely from LVT. Pittsburgh's Downtown Partnership (a BID) is also financed solely from LVT. Most of the PA split-rate cities have moved from being 'basket cases' to becoming prosperous again, in less than twenty years. Philadelphia meanwhile, as the largest city in PA and until recently fifth largest in the USA, persisted with the highest local wages tax in the country as it slid down the economic league table: city governors and property investors are now uniting in efforts to adopt split-rate and reduce wages tax.

Some fifteen mainland US states are at various stages of studying or adopting split-rate property tax laws: Virginia is the only one to have so far enacted a law and this was specially drafted to enable just one city – Fairfax – to adopt split-rate.

Hawaii adopted split-rate (locally known as 'graded tax') before most PA cities did, in 1963. Unusually it was a state tax but in 1978 property tax was devolved to local governments: for some reason only two counties retained the split rate.

Jamaica

British colonial administrators introduced LVT, as recently as 1957 in Jamaica and also in many of the other parts of West Indies, as a

19 There is no such requirement when reverting from split-rate to 'flat tax': several cities have increased tax revenue while scrapping split-rate overnight.

20 In Harrisburg PA, the state capital, approximately half of all properties are tax exempt. Despite this, the city is the showcase for US 'split rate' tax (City of Harrisburg 2006).

way to break up large land holdings and encourage both agricultural and urban development. The previous property tax, which was similar to that in Britain, was thought to penalize those who wished to improve their property. The reform proposal, made in 1952, was endorsed by the International Bank for Reconstruction and Development. However it was only made possible by a programme of full cadastral survey and valuation following independence, using experts from Australia.

Jamaican LVT is still known locally simply as 'property tax' and the change of tax base appears to have happened without fuss. It operates uniformly across Jamaica at the same rate for all land use classes – but with more valuable sites paying part of the tax at higher rates, rather like higher increments of earned income attract higher tax rates. This is seemingly to encourage sub-division of plots and incorporate an element of 'ability to pay', on the assumption that most high-value land is owned by wealthy people. Jamaica's property tax exhibits an exemplary provision for Relief Certificates in case of hardship, which allows an owner occupier to avoid payment until death or sale.

The full implementation of the site-value-based property tax was not made until valuation of all land was complete in 1977. Efforts to assess for and collect the tax were sensibly concentrated in high-value urban areas, where there was the greatest yield from that necessary investment. Currently the effective tax rate is around one percent of capital site value for a typical commercial site and 0.25% for a domestic site. It only accounts for about one percent of all revenues and although not explicitly hypothecated is generally regarded as 'for' property-related expenditure such as street lighting and waste disposal. Local politicians are generally supportive of the tax and would like to increase its yield while accepting that this would require more accurate site valuations.

Africa

As with the West Indies, in British Africa colonial administrators favoured site-value-based property taxes over what they themselves used back home: 'Do as I say, not as I do!' Kenya and South Africa present the most notable African implementations of LVT for local government. South Africa led the way as early as 1916 and by 1984 most cities had chosen to use SVR rather than the original British 'improved value' rating system.

Several other sub-Saharan Commonwealth countries allow local authorities to choose SVR but most poor countries lack the administrative infrastructure to ensure that sophisticated modern tax systems of any kind can operate. In Kenya, all local authorities have adopted SVR since the 1956 Act introduced a coherent property tax law. It accounts for nearly half the revenue collected by Nairobi City Council. However collection rates are very low: under 30% in some districts. Corruption of officials cannot be blamed on SVR: it applies in every area of government.

Namibia recently adopted a land tax as an explicit policy measure to encourage land reform, hoping to break up large farms owned by expatriates without resort to the methods of Mugabe in neighbouring Zimbabwe. Native owners pay a lower rate than expatriates.

The UK Policy Context

THE HISTORY OF LVT in Britain has already been touched upon (Connellan 2004). The policy is creeping up on politicians from every direction **except** the one that most matters: the doorstep and mailbag. Political history is not very helpful to them, because so much has changed about the context within which land and tax policies are nowadays formulated. The structures within which political debate takes place are hard to influence head-on in this complex area, with a diverse range of stakeholders, professions and points of policy that are impacted upon by change.[21]

Property taxes are mutually dependent on spatial planning and geo-information policies and techniques, so before devising any LVT implementation it is necessary to understand how such policies are themselves tending to develop. Those who advocate better use of location data for good governance need to work with others who advocate changes in property tax policy. Reasons for establishing more accurately the spatial pattern of values for land and other natural resources go far wider than property taxes. Value mapping – the art of monitoring and revealing the changes in value of any geo-spatial phenomena that have economic value – is just as capable of enabling tax reform as it is of being enabled by it.

Five factors appear to be influencing UK public policy in the area of property taxes:

- Devolution

21 The author has used a Policy Delphi to explore a large part of this policy landscape (Vickers *et al* 2005). This has helped clarify a set of potential policy actions that experts in a wide range of relevant fields have contributed to developing and which largely frames the conclusions of this book. A Delphi is a process for developing policy consensus in a complex field where many kinds of specialist knowledge require to be integrated and used for forecasting future possibilities, trends and responses to technical developments. Beginning in the defence field, it has spread to social and environmental sciences.

- Environmentalism (growing emphasis on sustainable development)
- EU enlargement
- Globalization
- Technology (especially spatial analysis techniques)

DEVOLUTION

Members of both the Scottish Parliament and Welsh Assembly and their government officials, despite being greatly constrained by their limited powers, desire to show their citizens that they are more effective and more inclined to consider new ideas than Westminster or Whitehall. It is noticeable that the swing against the incumbent UK Labour government in the 2005 general election was smaller in Wales and Scotland than in England, also that Liberal Democrat candidates did particularly well north of the Border, despite their Holyrood colleagues being part of a coalition with Labour, in power for six years. Lacking much of the historical baggage of the London establishment, devolved governments – including that of London itself – adopt new policies wherever they can.

In Scotland there is a specific public interest in land reform – *'the most distinctive area of Scottish policy'*, one former Labour MP[22] put it – and there are specific powers to alter both the method of local taxation and the amount raised. The Scottish Green Party made LVT one its five top campaign issues for the 2003 Parliamentary elections and went from one to six MSPs. The Lib Dems and Socialists supported SVR as replacement for Scottish business rates. Some MSPs of Labour and the Scottish Nationalist parties favour LVT too. That leaves only the Scottish Conservatives totally opposed and a majority of MSPs likely to favour a Tax Shift.

Wales has far fewer powers to vary taxation but the administration in Cardiff showed early on that it was prepared to use them, by scrapping the transitional arrangements[23] for business rates

22 Calum Macdonald (then MP for Outer Hebrides) at a conference of the International Union for LVT in 2001.

23 'Transitional arrangements' mean that changes in business rates that follow from five-yearly revaluations can, in England, take more than five years to be fully reflected in actual bills. Whilst this may please those whose property values have risen, it is unfair on those whose values have fallen.

which increase the regressivity of that tax. Where Welsh property values reduced in 2000 and 2005, business rates did as well – without the long delays which English firms suffer.

Devolution has helped to re-open the debate over how new UK-wide expenditure commitments are shared out between nations: the so-called Barnett Formula. Set before Scotland's offshore oil and gas fields boosted its economy, many believe this formula is generous to Scotland and unfair to England and – to a lesser extent – Wales. The Formula is based on a complex assessment of needs and the system overall could be made more equitable by having the UK's revenue raising based largely on relative land values: the huge land values in the City of London would contribute more; the more marginal 'Celtic fringe' lands considerably less. This would accord with the 'ability to pay' principle and logically lead to a similar formula being looked at for the allocation of central grants to English regions and/or local authorities.

Two principles should become clear which apply to all levels of government in the post-devolution debate over revenue sharing:

1 **Accountability**. A government that makes a decision to incur expenditure should pay for the cost of that decision and should also be able to decide how that revenue is raised.

2 **Beneficiary Pays**. Within the area affected by any expenditure, the costs – both direct and indirect – should be shared in accordance with the degree to which people benefit or are harmed by the decision that led to it.

The Scottish Parliament's Local Government Finance Review Committee Report (Burt 2006) was disappointing in respect of these principles, which it acknowledged as '*received wisdom*' and '*theoretical argument*' but found were hardly supported by opinion survey or other evidence. It concluded that the '*balance of funding*' issue was '*of little importance*'. However it did accept that wealth, as well as income, should be taxed by local government – with property '*a reasonable proxy for wealth*' – and it rejected Local Income Tax on the grounds that income was already taxed enough and property tax is more '*suitable for collection locally*'. Apart from that, the best that can be said of its work is that it provided a forum for devolved debate on a subject that all agreed to be urgent and important.

In a recent pamphlet on LVT, two academics from Oxford University who both support it expressed different views on whether it should be a tax for central or for local government (Maxwell and Vigor 2005). Iain McLean tends to agree with the Burt report view that a tax which is intrinsically geographic ought to raise revenue primarily for local government. John Muellbauer takes the more macro-economic view and would assign revenue from LVT mainly to HM Treasury. But neither would argue strongly against the above two principles.

In the Balance of Funding study (ODPM 2004)[24] and subsequent Lyons Inquiry (Lyons 2007)[25] – both looking at local government finance in England and Wales – the point was largely missed that the biggest cause of 'imbalance' between centrally assigned and locally raised revenues for councils is their over-dependence on a single property-based tax that takes little account of regional disparities in land values: council tax. Whilst UBR evens out geographic disparities in commercial property tax yields by being 'uniform' within each nation, it also helps exaggerate the inequalities between local areas' ability to raise similar amounts from the same CT rate. Local authorities are almost powerless to affect these inequalities which are a function of regional and local differences in land value. Moreover the present local finance system virtually ignores accountability and pays little attention to who really benefits from local expenditure whether it is centrally or locally authorised.

McLean (2005) points out that neither of the current property taxes meet any sensible test of justice or efficacy, especially under a

24 The Layfield Committee of 1975-6 looked more widely than Raynsford did at underlying principles of local government and explicitly recognised both the above principles. More recent studies have not clearly done so.

25 The British Retail Consortium (BRC) submission, quoted by Lyons in his final report, put the business case for LVT as a local tax:

> *'Land Value Tax (LVT) has a number of advantages. These include not distorting behaviour in the same way as taxes on income and profits do, LVT's potential effectiveness in incentivising the efficient use of land (as all land would incur a charge even when it was not being used for productive activity) and taxing land values could also enable local governments to profit from some of the increase in value as a result of a prosperous local economy.'*

devolved system. With the supposedly locally 'owned' council tax, an increase in tax base and revenue potential through increased population and/or prosperity results in reduced central government grant. With the Uniform Business Rate – 'nobody's tax' in McLean's words – any relationship between net revenue yield to an authority and its tax base is explicitly removed, except for a complex so-called Business Rate Growth Incentive scheme, at the margins.

Hardly anyone understands how Whitehall officials calculate each local authority's allocation from the central pot. However it is not necessary to understand the method in order to realise that any method which ignores changes over space and time in land values will fail to create a level playing field upon which councils' performance and locally levied tax levels can properly be judged. The funding game is bound to be rigged somehow unless and until the innate wealth-creating capacity of regions and local areas is accounted for: LVT is the best way to do that.

At every level of geography, high value land has the potential to generate higher earnings through rent (wealth for owners) and/or property taxes (revenue for governments). In order for one level of government to create a level playing field upon which lower tiers can play the economic game fairly, there needs to be a means of collecting revenue for that government's functions in accordance with the ability of each subsidiary area to pay. LVT is such a means, because it takes into account the *ab initio* yield potential of each such area as well as the consequent relative benefits to it.

Parish and town councils now can raise a precept to pay for any facility which they decide serves their people. So too should all devolved levels of government be able to levy LVT upon the landowning beneficiaries of projects which they have the duty or power to finance and provide.

At a regional level, an example might be the construction of a new air- or sea-port serving that region. The regional government would assess the cost of the scheme, discuss with neighbouring regions whether there is also a benefit to them (if there is, a contribution to costs being agreed) and then use a land-value based method of raising revenue that will yield the amount needed to pay for it. During the years that follow, sites near to the port will see their values generally increase much more than sites far removed. Some sites will suffer reduction in value, perhaps because they are near to approach roads which generate pollution but not near access points to those roads. LVT will account for these different degrees of benefit and harm, expressed through the property market, in an equitable manner.[26]

The same would apply to every decision made by that regional authority that has some effect on land values. Distinguishing between the effects of a particular scheme or decision upon particular site values and the effects of other actions is very difficult in an area which is subject to many tiers of government and also to the infinite numbers of decisions that private enterprise and other agencies make which impact upon site values in different ways and are themselves inter-dependent.[27] For this reason, in a multi-level democracy LVT is particularly appropriate as a form of revenue raising that can be used by each level of government on a devolved basis, applying the precepting tool already used in two-tier and parished areas of UK local government.[28] It overcomes the need to justify the 'fairness' of any expenditure that benefits one geographic community more than another: regular site assessments and a reasonably high rate of LVT take care of that.

To assist with deciding how far it would be right to go in using LVT as a revenue source for devolved multi-tier government, a simple distinction might perhaps be made between:

- expenditure on the **operation** of services, which is largely in the form of wages and consumables and could equitably (if not

26 This is similar to Tax Increment Financing (see below, page 78).

27 Transport for London (TfL) have concluded this in their studies of the impact of the Jubilee Line Extension (JLE) on land values. There is no doubt that the aggregate uplift in site values caused directly by this one investment project far exceeded its cost, even when limiting the study of its influence to quite a tightly defined area around the new stations. Despite the difficulty of accounting for the many other influences upon the areas studied, TfL believe it is possible to devise a reasonably fair hypothecated tax to pay for such a project. However more information needs to be collected routinely about property and used in spatial analysis to produce better tax assessments.

28 Precepting is widely used in other countries, saving administration costs by cutting out levels of administration. There is no reason why local government in general could not precept into national tax systems, including income tax (PAYE). Income tax could also include an element of Wealth Tax, as happens already in Sweden and the Netherlands. Combine the two and you have complied with the above two 'principles' while minimizing administration costs.

efficiently) be paid for by users and/or taxes on income and profits; and

- capital **investment** expenditure, which is what most reflects in land values, and hence should draw upon LVT.

The government which underwrites the capital investment should levy the LVT; the one which operates – or lets the franchises for – the transport service should decide what if any fare subsidy is appropriate and decide how to finance it.

In contrast to the USA and Australia, where historically powers have been devolved upwards from local communities through states to the federal government, the UK starts from a position where all power is held by Whitehall unless and until specifically devolved downwards. Any mention of having a tax policy piloted in Scotland touches a raw nerve, because UK Prime Minister Margaret Thatcher imposed the Poll Tax on pre-devolution Scotland without democratic consent. It is very different now, although even now it is a bold English resident who suggests that Scotland should try LVT before England has it: the initiative needs to come from within the community itself.

Whether or not LVT is best used as a national, regional or local tax (or any combination), it is first necessary for the UK Government to decide what (if any) use it wishes to make of the tax at its own level. It then needs to establish an infrastructure within which lower tiers can choose whether or not to use it, including statutory definitions of 'site value', standards and procedures for land information management, an appeal system, etc. Finally it needs to set out the parameters within which regions, nations and local authorities can levy this or any other modern property tax.

In summary, devolution is already happening and this has triggered a debate on how to share the available tax-raising powers at each level of government. It should also help bring LVT into that debate, especially since Liberal Democrats have been electorally successful within devolved administrations and, along with Greens and other minor parties, seem sympathetic to the policy. Every tier of government should be looked at together, especially revenue flows between tiers which should be minimised for the sake of accountability.

SUSTAINABLE DEVELOPMENT

Spatial planning policy is as much constrained as tax policy by the UK's top-down approach, wherein local planning authorities are largely servants of central government. However there is at least some scope for variation in the way that planning authorities can use statutory powers and hence some debate at all levels about what is meant by 'sustainable development'. When land taxes were last a major topic of political debate, this term was unknown and environmentalism was not conceived.

James Robertson, a founder of the New Economics Foundation (NEF), was commissioned by the European Commission Forward Studies Unit in 1997 to produce a concise reference book on the subject and despite resistance from some economists in the EC published it two years later, claiming the absence of LVT obstructs the efficient use of land (Robertson 1999). NEF itself published his 'Radical Strategy' on tax reform in 1994 (Robertson 1994), and he set out his philosophy in a collection of essays in 1998 (Robertson 1998) called ***Beyond the Dependency Culture***. In its Introduction he writes:

> *'A shift from dependency to co-operative self-reliance will be an essential feature of a successful transition to a post-industrial, post-modern age.'*

His basic thesis is that work and investment involving sustainable use of all natural resources have to be encouraged and that the tax and benefits systems are currently dysfunctional: *'The Devil himself could not have devised a worse system.'* So long as over a third of earned incomes and profits are taken away by government in tax, how can 'co-operative self-reliance' be achieved? Robertson supports introducing LVT alongside a Citizens Income, while phasing out income tax, VAT, NI and profits taxes.

The spatial planning policy debate is muddied by the plethora of QUANGOs (e.g. English Partnerships, Commission for Architecture and the Built Environment, Urban Development Corporations, Regional Development Agencies, largely unelected Regional Assemblies, newest of all the National Housing and Planning Advice Unit) that interfere (or assist, depending on your viewpoint) in spatial planning policy-making, funding and implementation. It is also confused by the high degree of dependence on state handouts, all ultimately at the expense of general taxation, which accompany every step in the process of trying to achieve sustainability. In a sense, this complexity and bureaucracy is itself unsustainable. The many policy 'wheezes' that Governments have for decades wheeled out in front of the development industry and public alike are never robustly audited for their effectiveness.

A number of respected organisations and individuals in the broad environmental movement have accepted that LVT is a potential tool for sustainable development. The latest surge in interest stems from John Prescott's appointment of international architect Richard (Lord) Rogers to investigate policies for urban renewal, early in 1998 (Rogers *et al* 1999).

The Town & Country Planning Association (TCPA), whose founder Ebenezer Howard was a follower of Henry George and which has always espoused policies that capture the elusive 'unearned increment', obtained funds from the Joseph Rowntree Foundation (JRF)[29] to probe such policies further than Rogers had done. TCPA commissioned a series of round-table discussions in late 1999, resulting in a report called ***A Taxing Question*** (Evans & Bate 2000). One of the report's five recommendations was that *'The Government should seriously examine the case for establishing a system of LVT in the longer term'.*

The Fabian Society report of its Commission on central/local government relations under Lord Plant, written by Michael Jacobs in 2000, had a whole chapter on LVT which concluded: *'today land taxation is more sensibly viewed as a form of environmental taxation'* (Jacobs 2000).

Friends of the Earth (FoE), in their 2001 commentary on likely Budget measures, for the first time explicitly called for LVT. The previous year FoE had helped set up The Progressive Forum (PF),

---

29 In Joseph Rowntree's Memorandum to his advisers on setting up a charitable trust in his name, written in 1904, he said: *'Every social writer knows the supreme importance of questions connected with the holding and taxation of land, but for one person who attempts to master this question there are probably thousands who devote their time and strength to relieving poverty and its accompanying evils. ... Such aspects of [the Land question] as the nationalisation of land, or the taxation of land values, or the appropriation of the unearned increment – all needs a treatment far more thorough than they have yet received.'*

along with Lord Plant and TCPA, to promote discussion and research on sustainable taxation. PF's first London event was a seminar chaired by NEF's Deputy Director and hosted by Transport for London (TfL), at which Robertson and American Green campaigner Alanna Hartzok were main speakers.

Given the demographic shift that is set to last across the developed world, failure to tax stored wealth in the form of houses owned by older non-working people while taxing incomes of the diminishing proportion of the population who create that wealth – and who are already over-burdened with personal debt, much of it housing-related – must be unsustainable. The 'feel-good factor' built on the frail back of house values makes economies appear healthy even as household spending bizarrely exceeds after-tax income, as it did in 2005 in the US for the first time since the Great Depression, '*eating the seed corn*' again (Harrison 2006): this time metaphorically but just as unsustainable. Any hiccup in the real economy would in this situation result in massive negative equity.

The rest of this section takes just a handful of existing or recently discarded policy tools from the fields of housing, regeneration, transport planning and agricultural policy to show briefly how perversely they operate and how the use of LVT could achieve their objectives more in accord with sustainable development.

Housing

Recent housing finance policy and wider economic policy have affected the housing market in a totally perverse way, so that in much of the country the only people who are able to enter that market unaided are those who do not need to. Without a loan from family, friends or mortgage lenders (or all three) amounting to twice what their parents needed – in real terms – to make that crucial first step onto the housing ladder, young families and single wage-earners are nowadays forced to rent.[30] More of the rented sector

30 'Intergenerational Equity' is a concept that can be extremely hard to incorporate into economic models. A better approach might be to deal with the pragmatic reality of having older and younger generations coexisting in a rapidly widening generational wealth gap. Is it politically wise or sustainable for governments to allow housing affordability to worsen, so that the young depend on '*parents both wealthy and generous*' (Muellbauer 2004, 5) to secure a basic human need: shelter?

than for over sixty years is owned by small investors, who sensibly (for them) capitalise on the desperation of lenders to create money by using their existing equity to buy-to-let much of the new stock that is built, thus keeping prices artificially high through speculation. Because there is little incentive to build – even after planning permission is granted – and every incentive to hold on to land, this artificial demand fails to trigger an increase in supply. It just raises land prices further. As well as adding to wealth disparities, this makes the housing market a potential source of extreme instability, as Muellbauer (2003) advised HM Treasury in a paper which was commissioned as part of preparations for UK joining the Euro zone.

Instead of the Blair Government using a range of fiscal tools to achieve sustainability in house prices, the boom in house prices has been exploited for short-term economic and political advantage: with manufacturing and other productive parts of the economy flat-lining, the economy is sailing along on a consumer boom backed by the 'feel-good' that home-owners associate with rising prices, coupled with record personal debt[31] across almost the whole of society. Low interest rates keep the housing market over-inflated, the pound high and hence encourage imports and depress exports and production. House purchase debt has risen, as a proportion of GDP in the UK, from 23% in 1980 to 72% in 2003, with loans now being commonly given amounting to ten times annual salaries of these vulnerable new borrowers (Harrison 2006).

The Bank of England has to use interest rate rises to dampen house prices with extreme care, because it could cause the consumer bubble to burst and take much of the economy with it. Muellbauer (2003) points out that LVT would result in low but more stable interest rates and would largely end land speculation, thereby dampening house price rises (and falls) and increasing the volume of new build.

---

31 Michael Rowbotham has studied the link between house (land) prices, personal debt and the wider economy in ***Grip of Death*** and ***Goodbye America!*** From the latter book (page 95): *'Not only do citizens in the UK own a smaller proportion of houses than 30 years ago and not only are there nearly four times as many mortgaged properties, but on those mortgaged properties people owe nearly twice as much in relation to their annual income ... In 1960, 19% of the total volume of UK private housing stock was under mortgage. By 1996, it was 37%.'*

As house prices and market rents rise on the back of speculation, an ever greater proportion of public expenditure on housing goes on benefits and land acquisition for social housing, rather than constructing new homes. But without an increased supply of affordable housing, the gap between the earnings level at which social housing can be accessed and that which is needed to buy without assistance increases. The so-called 'intermediate sector', in which 'key workers' acquire part of the equity in their properties, now takes a further bite out of available public expenditure on housing, none of which helps to create more houses but fuels effective demand and brings closer the prospect of the taxpayer having to bail out millions of people who have entered the market at unsustainable price levels. Yet many key worker housing schemes are so bureaucratic that new homes sit empty for months in areas desperate for nurses and teachers.

As Toby Lloyd of the Henry George Foundation pointed out at a recent conference on 'Building More Houses' (ironically nobody else actually spoke on the precise conference topic), there isn't actually a shortage of houses. The houses are simply in the wrong place – a '*northern unemployment problem*' – and many of them are under-occupied.[32] The stock of houses increases by only one or two percent a year, of which most are not affordable. As Lloyd says:

> *'The social housing sector currently makes up 21% of stock, a percentage falling every year. Almost 80% of houses are privately owned, 70% are owner-occupied. So why focus all our efforts to solve the housing crisis on a tiny minority of housing in a sector that is diminishing rather than on the bulk of them?'*

Add the estimated number of empty homes (700,000) to the number under-occupied (including 500,000 second homes) and you have the equivalent of at least ten years' of what Barker says

32 Muellbauer (2004) points out that a property tax linked to current market values is far more likely to improve effective supply of homes from existing stocks of under-used housing than any tax measure that merely affects new build, since there are 99 times as many units of existing stock than there are new units. To achieve the same effect on elasticity of housing supply, LVT's impact on existing home-owners need be only 1/100th as drastic as that of any measure focused on new build.

needs to be built to meet demand. In other words, we ought to be able – and need – to devise policies that bring **existing** houses onto the market to be occupied more appropriately, alongside any policies that might simply make more **new** houses affordable.

Making existing housing suitable for multi-occupation generally involves construction work that attracts VAT at 17.5%, whereas new build – including demolition of perfectly good homes to make way for flats – is zero-rated. So adoption of a flat-rate 5% VAT on all construction would go a long way to creating a level playing field for renovation and adaptation of housing stock, surely more sustainable in terms of re-use of land and materials than much of the small-scale redevelopment now being seen throughout southern England.

The so-called 'roof tax' in Milton Keynes, a variant on the Government's proposed tariff on new house-building, adds to the cost of new homes in the private sector. Whilst it does ensure essential infrastructure is provided for those homes, it loads all the costs onto only a minority of those who benefit from that infrastructure. When the new schools and health centres are built, the value of **all** homes in an area rises, whereas the price of only the newly built ones is burdened with the roof tax. Once again, a policy supposed to encourage affordable housing overwhelmingly benefits those who don't need their housing to be more affordable and actually helps makes the problem worse: perverse and unsustainable.

LVT quite simply ensures that all beneficiaries pay according to the amount they benefit, which is reflected in house (i.e. land) price movements. The Oxfordshire LVT study showed it to be a cheap and simple measure, especially as data revealing market fluctuations become more readily available. If the site valuations were adjusted according to market movements every year and were discrete and not banded like council tax assessments, not only would the housing market operate much better but LVT could actually lubricate the market, helping satisfy real housing need rather than speculative greed (Godden *et al* 2005).

Regeneration

Politicians love to interfere. Take them to a derelict inner city area and their first reaction is 'something must be done'. If they are in power and wish to retain the favour of voters in a deprived area, what they do next is throw money (invariably someone else's) at the problem, in the hope of claiming credit for a hoped-for 'solution'. Little do they know that one simple measure alone, which actually involves taking money **from** a small minority of voters – and no hand-outs – could be sufficient to ensure sustainable development of cities. As one modern American campaigner[33] puts it: *'LVT is regeneration without ribbon cutting'.*

Grants, awards and tax exemptions for areas in need of regeneration seem superficially to be the obvious answer. But the first thing that happens to such areas when even a hint of a major handout is given is a rise in land values, passed on to tenants as higher rents. This is well known in the property industry and beyond:

> *'In the 1980s when properties in enterprise zones were given a rate-free 'holiday', the observed effect for most properties in these zones was that rents rose.'* (Dixon 2000)

The day after the Olympics was awarded to London, the ***Evening Standard*** front page headline was:

> *'Gold Rush – Property Prices in Games areas set to soar by 50%'.*

If the unearned increment in land value is not made the subject of a tax, recycling it back to the government or wider community, there is nothing to stop the money supposedly going to regenerate the area leaving via the pockets of landowners who may be based somewhere else entirely and have done nothing to contribute to value uplift. That has been the experience of deprived areas like Liverpool.

The Nobel Prize-winning American economist William Vickrey said in 1991:

> *'Cities have the capacity to be fully self-financing without dependence on either federal assistance or on general taxes that are unrelated to benefits received.'*

33 Josh Vincent, Director of the Centre for the Study of Economics, Philadelphia, speaking at a conference on urban renewal in Bournemouth November 1999, paraphrasing an expression often used by Mayor Stephen Reed of Harrisburg PA, 2006 US Mayor of the Year.

The condition for this self-sufficiency or sustainable **re**-development was, he said (Giacalone and Cobb 2001), to reform the property tax and replace it with LVT:

> *'The property tax combines one of the best and one of the worst taxes we have. The portion that falls on sites or land values is the only major tax that is reasonably free of distortionary effects and is not intolerably regressive.'*

The city leaders of Brisbane in 1987 commissioned a report on whether their existing LVT should be retained. When their Committee of Inquiry reported eighteen months later, it concluded that ...

> *'the benefit principle rather than ability-to-pay was the most equitable and rational basis of public revenue-raising ...'*

and moreover that ...

> *'a tax or rate levied on property – provided it is levied on land and not upon the buildings or other visible improvements erected on the land – is the basic general revenue source which most nearly conforms to the benefit principle'*

because it ...

> *'encourages development and discourages the speculative withholding of vacant land from productive use ...'*
>
> (Brisbane City Council 1989)

The Committee rejected all forms of tax other than LVT, noting that:

- poll tax was regressive and expensive to operate;
- local income tax would tax some residents who did not earn their living in the city and not tax some who work there but live outside, hence not be in accord with the beneficiary principle; and that
- all consumption taxes would be inherently inflationary and unrelated to benefits received from city services.

A recent study of local taxes used by over 200 cities in Pennsylvania (PA) – all but about 20 of which did not use split-rate –

showed a strong correlation between successful regeneration, measured by value of construction starts, and the extent to which LVT was used. The least successful city in terms of retaining its wealth and population was Philadelphia, which has the highest local income tax in the USA and is tightly circled by centres of employment avoiding its wage tax. Every 1% Tax Shift off buildings and onto land values in PA seems to correspond to a 16% increase in construction, other things being equal (Plassman & Tideman 1999). It was this 'mixed model site value rating' which attracted Lord Rogers' interest in his report for the Urban Task Force in 1999, wherein he called for further studies of it as possibly the most effective policy for urban renewal.

In framing legislation for Business Improvement Districts (BIDs) in the 2003 Local Government Act, the UK Government stubbornly set its face against a move towards LVT, which is used to entirely finance the centre-city BID in Pittsburgh PA.[34] Despite there being wide support for a BID levy that extended to property owners, Government steadfastly denied BIDs the right to choose any compulsory levy other than a supplement to non-domestic rates (NDR), because NDR – unlike American property taxes – is levied on occupiers and not owners. Some effects are bizarre, such as:

a Outside businesses which invest in a BID are denied a vote in its affairs;

b Businesses pay for the BID three times over: first in a BID levy; then, as the BID's success drives rents up, to their landlord on rent review; finally, at the next NDR revaluation, in a higher base NDR.

British legislation on BIDs flies in the face of what makes this regeneration idea a success elsewhere: the involvement of property owners.[35] If the interests of owners are not tied in with those of occupiers, it exaggerates the unsustainable features of existing UK

34 Muellbauer (2004,16) states that LVT *'automates the mechanism by which US BIDs are used to finance infrastructure'*. Pittsburgh is actually the only US BID that uses LVT but all property taxes in the US are levied on owners, not occupiers, so they contain an element of 'incentive taxation' to promote renewal.

35 In Scotland, Parliament listened to appeals from the British Property Federation and incorporated landowners' contributions into BIDs legislation.

policies. With BIDs it is local entrepreneurs rather than the general taxpayer at local or national level who are subsidizing owners. The tax burden has shifted further the wrong way: off owners onto occupiers.

There is just a glimpse of hope in two things which Minister Lord Rooker said at the time he rejected an owners' levy:

> *'Any mandatory levy on property owners would be defined as a new tax, a significant change to our current local taxation system [and therefore] very difficult to justify for the sake of BIDs alone ... If we see substantial evidence that BIDs are failing because property owners are not included on a mandatory basis, then we shall consider ways that that situation can be rectified.'*
>
> (Hansard 16 July 2003, House of Lords, Col.920)

A review of BIDs legislation began in 2006 and runs until late 2008, so the argument for allowing land owners to fund regeneration through BIDs could be heard again soon. Since the Conservatives supported Lib Dems and others in seeking the owners' BID levy option, it will be harder for them not to support SVR if Government accepts the Lib Dems' policy on taxing commercial land, which was seen in its latest urban policy paper as *'a vital element of our regeneration strategy'*:

> *'By taxing the value of land itself in its best permitted use, rather than on the value of any buildings on the land, SVR provides the right incentives to promote regeneration' ...*
>
> (Liberal Democrat Party 2000)

If SVR has such advantages in terms of regeneration in commercial parts of cities, why not apply those advantages to residential areas? The answer presumably lies in politics, not in economics or sustainability theory. Such a distinction between residential and non-residential land and tax policy is an obstacle to sustainable spatial planning, since it complicates the treatment of one of the most sustainable forms of urban renewal: live-work mixed development.

As for the social aspect of regeneration, it is totally predictable that those who see no hope in gaining a share of the plunder will vent their frustration in wanton vandalism. Rowntree (note 29, page 44) was right: we need to tackle the cause, not the symptoms.

Transport planning

Some of the most cogent thinking about 'good' and bad' sources of revenue has been done recently in the transport field. The European Conference of Ministers of Transport (ECMT) set out its principles for reforming transport taxes in 2003, starting with a 'tripartite' classification of taxes which applies to any field of public investment:

- Welfare positive: *'Taxes that enhance overall social welfare – taxes on externalities;*
- *'Taxes that are welfare-neutral – taxes on economic rents';* and
- Welfare negative: *'Taxes that reduce welfare – taxes on final consumption, on capital and labour, and a fortiori – on intermediate products.*

  It follows that, other things being equal, revenues foregone as a result of the failure to tax externalities and economic rents will require recourse to revenues from welfare-reducing taxation.'

  (ECMT 2003)

Welfare-reducing taxes in transport include VAT – not just on the fare itself but on everything that a transport operator buys to produce the service and income and profits taxes on transport workers and companies. Fuel duty and purchase tax on new cars are also welfare-reducing for the private motorist. However inasmuch as most types of fuel cause pollution, fuel duty can be regarded as welfare-positive, since in its absence there would be a modal shift towards single occupancy cars with possibly higher fuel consumption, as in the USA where road transport accounts for 11% of the world's entire petrochemical consumption.

A better way to tax pollution would be to impose fuel taxes 'upstream' (at the point where the raw petroleum is extracted) grading the tax according to the inherent 'dirtiness' of the source and also of the refined products. Pollution is not the only 'externality' caused by transport and generally is taxed insufficiently. Congestion, noise and abandoned cars are also externalities, the last of which the EU is moving towards internalising, through regulation, in the purchase price.

Welfare-neutral taxes on economic rents include all forms of user charge for that significant portion of land used by transport: parking fees; congestion charging; charging for airport landing slots and mooring fees. But land beyond that directly allocated to transport also receives benefit from it, through the connectivity of transport networks making some locations more favoured with economic activity than others. This is why LVT has particular relevance to transport planners.

Reliance on welfare-negative taxes distorts the wider economy and leads to perverse and unsustainable behaviour by rational human beings. It is almost universally accepted that the reliance upon private cars – and particularly 'gas-guzzling' varieties – in developed countries is one of the least sustainable features of modern life. It is not so well known that LVT derived from existing and future transport infrastructure could eliminate all forms of welfare-negative tax in this sector, and still leave a surplus revenue to help reduce general taxes.

In the UK, the debate on LVT in the transport sector was stimulated by the book ***Taken for a Ride***, by a South London property developer, Don Riley. His rough calculations were based on transactions in property during the construction of the Jubilee Line Extension (JLE) of which he personally had knowledge. They showed that land values within just a kilometre of the ten new stations rose by about 400% or £10bn over and above the construction and other costs of building the JLE, compared to the general rise of land values in that part of London. Subsequent independent studies, some with access to official data on VOA property valuations and/or confidential transaction data provided by property agents, have confirmed this.

Dr Rana Roy, a transport economist who advises the independent Railway Forum, has calculated that if all forms of welfare-positive and welfare-neutral taxes – what he calls 'optimal transport pricing' – were adopted (**excluding** LVT), there would be an increase in revenue from all forms of UK inland transport of some

£25bn per year. In other words, scrap all forms of fuel tax, taxes on vehicle purchase and use and replace them with highly differentiated road, parking space and track user charging. The result, he says, would be a 54% reduction in air pollution and CO^2 emissions from transport, as car traffic falls and motorists switch to less polluting vehicles. In Greater London, there would be a 20% reduction in car traffic and large increases in bus and train use, even without increased capacity of public transport. The new taxes would replace the current £40bn a year raised by all existing forms of revenue within the sector and leave over half as much again for the Chancellor to use in mitigating other non-transport taxes.

Roy goes on in a later paper for the Railway Forum ***Not by Spending Alone*** to look at how to use LVT to enable the necessary expansion in all public infrastructure (rail is just a highly visible subset of the overall problem) without adding to general welfare-negative taxes. He points out that even with the significant headline increase in annual public investment by the Labour Government since 1997, in real terms the shortfall in what is needed to maintain – let alone enhance – publicly funded infrastructure has risen from £28bn inherited from the Major Government to £70bn in 2004. So dysfunctional has been the method adopted for financing infrastructure that after ten years in power, the best that can be said for New Labour is that they have slowed down the rate at which public infrastructure such as railways is getting worse. Carrying on this way is clearly unsustainable. There is absolutely no prospect, with present policies, of closing the funding gap.

Using data from Denmark (because the UK Government cannot or will not make the equivalent data on our own land available) Roy estimates the potential land rent available to be collected as around 7.5% of total GDP,[36] which converts, at a LVT tax rate of 90%, to some £75bn per year. This is about twice what is now collected from all existing property taxes. This windfall, repeated every year, would be available **in addition** to that from reform of transport industry taxes (Roy 2004).

With Transport Minister Alistair Darling's announcement of road charging in 2005, it seems that the Government may be at last

36 GDP itself increases under a welfare-neutral tax regime.

grasping radical tax reform lifelines. However it is generally thought that the technical problems with all but the crudest forms of road charging, which requires dispersed new infrastructure such as GPS receivers in every car, are far greater than for LVT. In the time it would take to implement road charging, the infrastructure funding gap will not have closed. In any case, road charging is not designed to finance investment in other forms of transport so much as to disperse congestion on roads.

The Treasury is looking for Alternative Funding Mechanisms (AFMs), particularly in the transport sector. It will find more problems with every other AFM than it should find in LVT, for reasons that will be explained in more detail later. The main reason to signal a move towards LVT would be to enable finance for transport and other infrastructure to be secured from the bond markets **now**, against the collateral of a future revenue stream from welfare-enhancing LVT.

Agriculture

Just as Don Riley's book caught the public's attention because it seemed superficially like 'a turkey voting for Christmas', so has a book (Pickard 2004) on EU farm subsidies. Duncan Pickard is a farmer calling for an end to the Common Agricultural Policy (CAP) gravy train and for land to be taxed.

With agriculture as with housing, a large part of tax revenue is accounted for by benefit payments: cut the benefits and you cut taxes. All benefits interfere with free market operations and most benefits have perverse effects, as do tax exemptions. Therefore much of the perversity of the current tax system lies in its use in support of anti-market benefit payments.

What the CAP has done, with subsidies initially to production and since 2005 to land management, is to make the mere possession of agricultural land an entitlement to subsidy. Whether through a livestock head-count, yield- or area-based payments, it has grossly distorted the balance as against inputs of both labour and **true** capital. These subsidies pay the rent, pushing land prices up beyond the means of tenant farmers (because owners receive subsidies, not tenants) and making farm expansion attractive to owners and investors who often have no interest or expertise in production or sustainable land management. Agricultural land prices have long borne little relationship to farm-gate prices for produce, almost entirely thanks to the CAP regime.

The superficially attractive option of giving tenant farmers the right to buy their land, in the absence of tax reform and an end to farm subsidies, would have a similar effect to that which the 'right to buy' policy had on tenanted council housing: it would merely allow more farmers unjustly to share the unearned gains available from the CAP. As Pickard says:

> *'Subsidised farming is, by this[37] definition, not sustainable. Farming will never become sustainable without tax reform to get rid of the burden of high fixed costs.'*

Pickard is not so much in favour of taxing land (through LVT) as of removing the deadweight burden of existing taxes that make it artificially uneconomic to employ the labour that environmentally friendly farming and sustainable rural communities need. He cites Banks (2001), who estimated this burden at £14,500 per year per head of population.[38] These taxes are borne by the farmer, not the landowner. They encourage the laying off of farmhands, discourage new entrants to farming, make the application of capital-intensive methods more profitable than labour-intensive farming, disadvantage organic producers and generally reduce the earning capacity of farm **businesses** as opposed to the asset value of the farm **land**.

Although farmland represents about 85% of the land area of Britain, it accounts for less than 5% of its value. The burden of UK-wide LVT would therefore fall overwhelmingly on urban areas and not on owners of farm land. Just as farm rents rose as a result of agricultural land being de-rated in the 1920s, so would the introduction of LVT have a corresponding effect of depressing farm rents: all taxation is at the expense of rent. This would encourage owners to sell to tenant farmers, as the only way of passing on the new tax. Providing the reduction in other taxes more than matched

37 Pickard's dictionary defines 'economic sustainability' as *'prolonged survival without regular outside financial support'.*

38 The burden is not spread evenly among the population but is carried largely by employers and businesses, through income tax, national insurance, VAT, etc.

the new LVT, farmers would have greater incentive to invest and produce the goods and services that consumers want rather than those which attract subsidy. Marginal land would by definition attract no LVT but the reduction in other taxes would bring land that is currently uneconomic to farm back into profit. Agricultural land values at what is now the margin would rise.

The threat to British farming was heightened by accession of ten new members to the EU. Although at first the new accession states only receive 25% of the subsidy that Britain and the other 'old' member states receive per hectare, the relative size of the CAP within the EU total budget does not change, so that there has been an immediate impact on farm/land incomes throughout the EU. With the new member states reaching 100% per ha by 2013, without a dramatic fall in production costs (such as tax) many farmers will cease trading by then. The trend towards larger farms, with over-stretched owner-occupiers, will grow. Land will be left idle and poorly managed. However EU enlargement also offers an opportunity to 'grasp the nettle' of EU tax reform.

EU ENLARGEMENT

Just as devolution has 'unfrozen' the established way of thinking in many policy areas and hence provided an opportunity for LVT to be considered as a means of financing new institutions, so has the enlargement of the EU forced member states and the EC to look at how it finances itself. The new member states have had to make the most adjustment, especially those that emerged recently from Communism and had to re-learn market economics at a state level. However all member states now have an opportunity to review the 'balance of funding' between national and supra-national functions and governments.

Many of the former Communist countries of central and eastern Europe had forms of LVT in place or being implemented prior to being absorbed into the Soviet Block in the twentieth century. Among them Hungary, Poland, the Czech Republic, the Baltic States and Russia itself inherit a folk memory of Henry George's ideas that is far more relevant to them as they move from a centrally planned economy with little private ownership of land. The New Europe, as George W. Bush has noticed, is in some ways more open to free market ideas than the original EU states. LVT was linked in Henry George's thinking to Free Trade and cannot operate within a Communist framework, because there is no basis for valuing land if it is all state owned and largely occupied by state-run enterprises who pay no rent.

Among the first things that all these former Communist states have had to do is establish new land laws and property market institutions. Another early act within their legislatures was to frame tax laws. It was clear to most that there was a link between land and tax policies and that by taxing land they could provide themselves with a sustainable revenue stream while simultaneously creating a healthy property market. An open letter to Gorbachev (quoted in Schaefer 2004) from a bevy of economists in 1990 suggested LVT as a source of revenue: among those who spotted it was a young journalist called Chris Huhne, later an MEP and now Liberal Democrat MP for Eastleigh.

This 'clean slate' approach to basic elements of governance can be infectious, shaking the complacency of more mature states in Western Europe. The examples of the Baltic States are set out above and Britain could – and should – learn from them, particularly in dispelling some myths about the yield, effects and acceptability of LVT: the Flat Tax is not the only tax reform from 'the east' that should impact on the whole EU.

Having said that, every country is different and no property tax can be copied completely by one from another. Where there perhaps might be a more fruitful exchange of views and sharing of systems is at the supra-national level. The current debate among member states about burden sharing, rebates and multi-speed development towards 'closer Union' should be extended into the area of how the EU budget might be funded. A 'Europe Tax' which was based upon the relative wealth of nations as expressed in land value might be much fairer and able to support sustainable Europe-wide economic growth than VAT, which is a welfare-negative tax.

For reasons of environmental policy, the EC has directed that member states move towards a common structure for land information. The draft Directive originally included land values within the overall basket of attributes that need a common definition and forms of data exchange. The UK objected to this, so value is now not in the INSPIRE Directive, ratified in late 2006. This would have much greater impetus and also wider environmental benefits if LVT were to be adopted instead of the welfare negative VAT as the EU's tax, thereby requiring a pan-European land valuation.

It may be no coincidence that the conceptual term 'landvaluescape' has first found expression outside its inventor's publications in an EU document about the protection of coasts from erosion (Vickers *et al* 2006). If land values were shown as peaks in a 3D model, the landvaluescape of Europe would have its summit very close to Brussels and subsidiary peaks in the very areas from which net contributions need to flow if the European Project is to succeed. If Europe wants to protect its farmers, one way to do that is to protect the land they farm from the massive increase in value which results from allowing fields to be built on.

GLOBALISATION

The massive increase in value of farmland in the accession states of the EU which accompanied the extension of CAP subsidies is one aspect of a wider pattern of globalisation in trade. The same corporations and owners of large farms in Britain and other Western European countries that are buying up cheap land in Poland and other accession states of central and eastern Europe, indirectly at the expense of taxpayers in the rest of Europe who finance agricultural subsidies, are beneficiaries of the dumping of farm produce on countries outside the EU, North America and Japan. The losers are small farmers in the developing world, often unable to securitise the value of the land they occupy (because they lack title to it) and almost always unable to compete with multi-national producers of cash crops who destroy their local food markets at our expense and then buy up the land.

It is beyond the scope of this book to explore the impact of rich world farm subsidies on poor countries.[39] However one consequence is that the exemption from land taxes that has been achieved by

39 See ***Goodbye America!*** by Michael Rowbotham (2002 pp.139-140) for a brief explanation of how Third World debt links to globalization, Rich World farm subsidies and 'debt-for-equity swaps' enabling banks to mop up vast stores of natural resources and land – all virtually untaxed – at fire sale prices.

landowners in most of those rich countries over centuries is becoming prevalent elsewhere over mere decades. Dysfunctional tax systems are in danger of becoming global and will have disastrous effects on economic justice, biodiversity, sustainable communities and world peace. The fragile administrative infrastructure and ecosystems of much of the developing world cannot cope with the pace of change in land use and population movement: taxes go uncollected and laws that should protect the environment are flouted for lack of the capability to monitor them.

But globalisation is not all bad news. One consequence of the free flow of investment capital is the demand from shareholders of multinationals that assets are valued consistently. With up to 40% of the value of such companies being attributable to real estate and natural resource holdings, it is essential that a valuation of oil reserves in Alaska is done by the same method as one in Kazakhstan, that a site acquired for office development in Vilnius is valued comparably to one in Valparaiso. The desire of developing nations to attract foreign investment helps drive progress towards free property markets, which in turn demands that land cadastres are prepared, maintained and made freely available to market players.

The growth in demand for international comparability in investment property information has disturbed the complacency of British and European valuers. The International Valuation Standards Committee (IVSC) has decreed, in the Basle Accord of 2002, that property assets are valued for such purposes at market value, not current use value. This is to prevent asset-stripping by predators who plunder companies owning sites where, for example, obsolete protected manufacturing capacity has depressed the existing use value (EUV). As RICS put it in their submission to the UK Treasury:

> *'It is essential that internationally active banks, whatever countries they operate in, value their property collateral on a consistent basis. Without this, there can be no level playing field for capital adequacy worldwide.'* (Craig 2004)

Ironically the UK's own valuation profession has obtained a temporary opt-out from the new IVSC standard. Companies based in the UK can choose to continue with EUV for their British property, arguing that the British property market is still too opaque to allow them to assess HABU (i.e. market value) with sufficient accuracy. This could allow foreign companies who use modern valuation standards and methods to asset-strip British ones who don't.

Britain has very successfully aided the imposition of globalization on the rest of the world, until recently without seemingly wanting to expose its own land markets to the cold wind of free trade. As an institution without parallel in its involvement with global land and property markets, RICS is better placed than any to expound on the role land plays in globalization. In ***Land Markets and the Modern Economy***, distinguished fellows of RICS explained:

> *'Human populations are expanding, but the land is a finite resource, putting ever-increasing pressure on living-space.'*
> (Dale, Mahoney & McLaren 2002)

Far from land becoming **less** important as people move to cities, land and natural resources have **increased** in value both absolutely and relative to other forms of wealth and sources of income, as global prosperity and trade have increased. Even without growth in prosperity, land values grow as populations grow. The creation of active land markets both releases that value and accelerates its growth, the more so if the markets are global. But if land value is not largely recycled as revenue, gross distortions in wealth distribution occur. For property taxation of any kind, there needs to be an active land market to provide evidence in support of regular tax assessments.

A pre-condition for active land markets is a national land information service, underpinned by a geospatial data infrastructure using modern technology to manage and reveal to market players the changing status of land use, ownership and value.

TECHNOLOGY

Those currently at the top of the valuation, tax administration and political professions have witnessed huge advances in information processing and communications technologies late in their careers.

These advances have had a greater impact on LVT than on most forms of taxation. It may be uncomfortable to some senior property and tax professionals to know that technology has made much of their painfully acquired experience and skills redundant. However sooner or later those coming up through the ranks with knowledge of what is possible will lose patience with obsolete methods that waste precious resources – and with senior colleagues who obstruct progress through their inertia.

Whereas other taxes merely employ spreadsheet computations, modern property taxation can also make use of Automated Valuation Methods (AVMs), involving spatial analysis and map displays. If enough is known about specific plots of land, buildings, owners, occupiers and the transactions involving them, then using AVMs (also known as Computer-Aided Mass Assessment or CAMA) it is now relatively easy to derive local values for a large number of spatially variable components of the raw 'value' of each attribute. For example, a double garage may be worth more to someone buying a house in an area with a high residents parking charge than to someone in a green belt. If enough is known about all the property transactions in a tax jurisdiction area – **and** about properties that may **not** have come on the market recently – then geographically-weighted multiple regression (GWR) analysis can 'solve' for the local value of all variables (Gloudemans 2002). Having solved for everything tangible and man-made – from the value of good insulation to the value of a third bedroom, the 'residual' left over is the intrinsic value of a site: its 'location benefit' or 'common wealth' resulting from natural and communal characteristics that owe nothing to its owner. This is what is required for LVT.

In the past, even if all the necessary information about land and property was routinely collected, it was a very tedious manual task to produce site valuations without direct evidence of bare land sales in a locality. That was perhaps the main reason for claiming that LVT was impractical. Despite this, we have seen that many countries have managed to introduce and sustain LVT before technology made it much easier. Just as we administered income and sales taxes adequately when quill pens were the only tools available, so we managed to operate LVT before computers were invented. The computer technology used for income tax and VAT matured about ten years earlier than that needed to exploit spatial technology fully for LVT. However in the last ten or so years, massive increases in processing power have made it possible not only to make extraordinarily complex spatial calculations but to transmit pictures of their results instantly. This has made LVT not just cheap but transparently so.

In Britain, for historical reasons we start with a major disadvantage in not having the necessary information – either at all, or not in suitable form, or not freely available. Unlike most developed countries, we do not maintain inventories of buildings: we do not know which houses have insulation, which have double garages or even, in many cases, the material used for their construction. Some public agencies may possess part of the necessary information for part of the country but none has a reason to collect and maintain comprehensive datasets of this kind.

Thanks to the EU's INSPIRE Directive, this may soon change. Most of the attributes relating to buildings will be included, especially if they have a potential impact upon sustainability: for example, their energy consumption rating, which is a function of quality of insulation and materials used in construction, may need to be collected. INSPIRE may provide the regulatory stimulus for us to obtain all the information needed to derive land value, even if it does not oblige us to monitor value itself.

Technology can help with data collection, as well as with computation. Remote sensing by satellite or digital aerial photography is already part of the palette of products that OS provides, hitherto free to other central government agencies but for a price to the private sector. Satellites and aircraft can carry heat sensors that show whether a building is insulated or unoccupied, or infra-red sensors to reveal how bio-diverse a piece of woodland is. For those attributes which are not amenable to automated data collection, self-completion by building owners should be made more reliable by their realisation that the more information about what the owner has invested in a site is known by the authorities, the less likely the site itself will be over-taxed. Since LVT discounts what is man-made, why should an owner not declare 'improvements' in full? Quite apart from this incentive to volunteer property data, the introduction of Home Information Packs (HIPs) will mean that such data is eventually centrally held on all domestic properties that change hands in England and Wales.[40]

In countries that have already collected inventories of buildings and property transactions, it has been found that the property market itself works much better with the benefit of access to this data. For example, Lucas County Ohio provides free on-line access to its Assessors Real Estate Information System (AREIS) and for $10 supplies a CD-ROM with the entire history and up-to-date description of over 150,000 properties, complete with aerial photography and contour maps. When the on-line AREIS service was provided with a map base, there was a step change in the difference between what vendors offered as sale price for homes and the final price: the gap almost halved. Buyers could view all adjacent property records and most of the guesswork was taken out of negotiations, so much so that when the system goes down the switchboard at Lucas County offices is jammed. The Assessors Office itself believes that the quality of its tax assessments improved significantly because people were able to tell them about mistakes, just by observing the local pattern of recent transactions. A smoothly operating property market, as well as benefiting from advanced technology used by public authorities, feeds back positively into the work of those officials.

Whilst Lucas County does not have LVT, it has all the technical capacity to introduce it. LVT would benefit from and be of benefit to these advances in what is called Value Mapping. In a recent global survey of developments in Value Mapping (Vickers *et al* 2005), it was found that it seems to go hand-in-hand with moves to modernize property tax systems, which in turn tend to be accompanied by reforms involving more frequent and transparent revaluations and separation of land and building value. The relevance of frequent revaluations to acceptability and efficiency of property taxes has been explained already.

It is not claimed that technology can automate every property tax assessment. A rough guide is that 10% of properties, over-

40 However the officials responsible for introducing HIPs, when asked by the author in June 2006, not only said they have no plans to use this information for other purposes but that they would prevent it so being used.

whelmingly non-domestic ones, require individual assessment by a qualified valuer. What technology does is to free up the scarce skilled human resources of a tax assessment system to concentrate on achieving high quality valuations in the more difficult cases, because the vast majority of assessments can now be done far better with the aid of computers (see Denmark above).

Finally technology can remove much of the mystique of property taxes and help taxpayers to understand why they should pay what is being demanded. 'Landvaluescape' is a reality that, for British taxpayers until now, has been obscured by deficiencies in data and processing systems, also by a culture of secrecy and 'big brother knows best' that is alien to a modern democracy, particularly one where most people invest their life savings in property.

~ LVT and 'Taxing Differently' ~

THE DEFINITION of LVT given earlier explicitly says that it is regarded by its advocates as a tax to replace, not supplement, other taxes. The transport section explains how some taxes add to general welfare and others subtract from it, with LVT as welfare neutral. Before looking at (and then discarding) various forms of 'land tax' that are often put forward as easier options than LVT, the overall scope of Tax Shifting that is possible should be spelt out.

In a paper for Centre for Reform, Hinnells and Potter (2001) list a number of taxes that are qualitatively different in their economic and environmental effects from most existing taxes used in the UK. SVR was, in their view, capable of raising more revenue than any new tax except 'Total Energy Tax'. This was without extending its coverage beyond commercial land. The total Tax Shift potential was £91bn per year (28% of all revenue), of which SVR accounted for £27bn (30% of Tax Shift).

These figures are an adequate first-order estimate and the other Hinnells and Potter taxes are suitable components of an overall Tax Shift strategy. However many are welfare positive and not primarily designed to raise significant amounts of revenue or to remove the huge amounts of deadweight burden to the economy that LVT, as a welfare neutral tax, can do. Most environmental taxes cannot be relied upon to sustain public revenues, since they are primarily there to deter 'bad' behaviour and to erode their own tax base (e.g. tobacco tax is supposed to lead to less smoking, therefore less tobacco sold). In the Liberal Democrats' recent proposals (Liberal Democrat Party 2006), some of these taxes formed 40% (£8.1bn) of the ***Green Tax Switch***.

This ***Green Tax Switch*** could be regarded as extremely modest, accounting for only some 5% of total UK tax revenue. Proposals drawn up for Pacific Northwest America in 1996 (Durning and Bauman 1998) suggested that over a 10-year period it should be possible to reduce the proportion of welfare negative taxes on production and enterprise in their three states to under a quarter of the total raised, from around a half. As the charts below show, this is a part of the world that had already adopted, ten years ago, considerably more 'green' taxation than the UK.

Pacific Northwest America

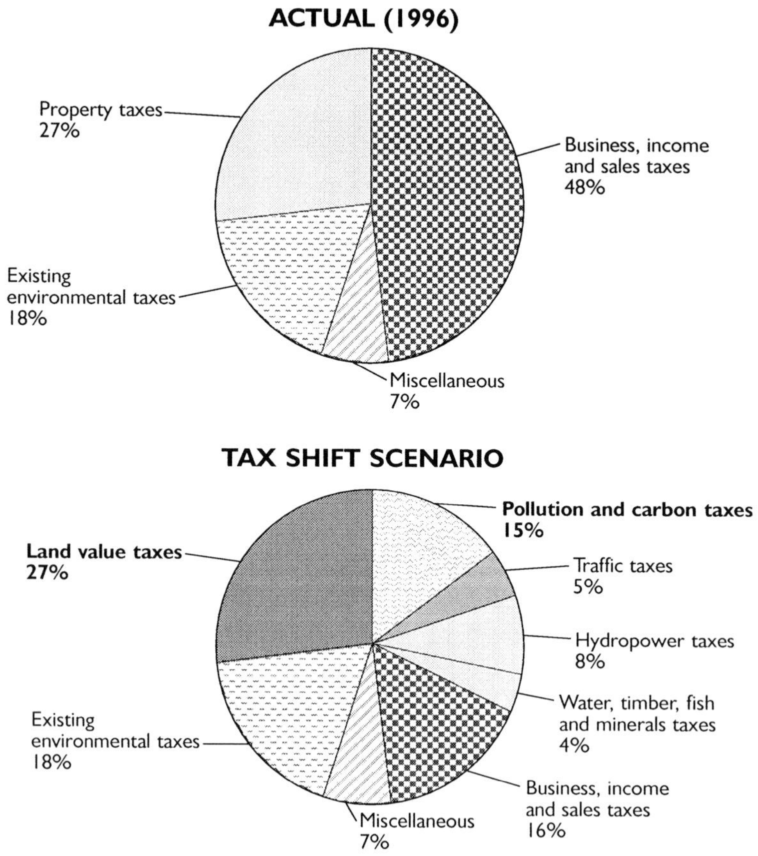

Source: Alan Thein Durning & Yoram Bauman, *Tax Shift* (Northwest Environment Watch, 1998).

Dead-End ‘Land Tax’ Options

AT VARIOUS TIMES, politicians and others who claim to understand the ethical and economic advantages of ‘land taxes’ over other policies for financing infrastructure, boosting housing numbers or helping promote ‘sustainable communities’ have proposed taxes other than LVT. Before focusing on how to introduce LVT to Britain, it is therefore necessary to make clear why other ‘land taxes’ are either counter-productive or short-term palliatives that cannot address the underlying problems to any significant extent.

There are two categories of ‘dead-end’ land tax options: one-off taxes; and *ad valorem* ‘modernised rates’. Within each category, several varieties under different names and with slightly different characteristics exist in the literature or even in practice. Both categories are largely tapping into the same source of revenue: the ‘unearned increment’ in land value, or economic rent of land. To avoid double taxation, any implementation of LVT should aim to reduce and eventually eliminate all these other ‘land taxes’ (if they already exist) before looking to other taxes that might be ameliorated.

HM Treasury has been using the expression ‘Alternative Funding Mechanisms’ (AFMs) in the context of financing the gap between the money needed to maintain infrastructure investment and what is currently earmarked from existing taxes. Most AFMs are land taxes. The danger of using LVT for gap funding has been mentioned. It is therefore to be hoped that LVT will not be explicitly adopted as an AFM in this context but as an alternative form of general taxation. Although several of the measures/AFMs covered below may serve a short-term purpose while LVT is brought in as a long-term measure, the danger is that by introducing them the Government may be lulled into thinking that they have solved a problem when they have merely postponed the solution.

ONE-OFF LAND TAXES

These include Betterment Levy, Development Land Tax, Development Charge, Land Premium, Tariffs, Planning Gain and Planning Gain Supplement, Capital Gains Tax, Impact Fees, Stamp Duty Land Tax, Inheritance Tax and Green Field Development Tax and Community Land Auctions.

Betterment Levy was introduced by the Labour Government in 1967 and levied (initially at 40% of the 'development value') when land was sold, leased or its value realized by 'material development'. Like the 100% **Development Charge** which preceded it (from 1947 to 1952), it was payable by the owner at the time that 'betterment' (of land value) occurred, so it relied on owner action. Since owners correctly forecast that a Conservative Government would repeal these measures, the vast majority of owners of developable land were reluctant to part with it so long as Labour remained in power. The land market dried up, land prices actually rose (supply and demand) and receipts from Betterment Levy were far less than expected. The **Development Land Tax** (DLT) of 1976 showed that Labour hadn't learned the lesson: tax an event and you deter it. Set at 80% of the gain in value realized by developers, its authors seemed to think that a few more exemptions, allowances, conditions and special cases – and 95 pages of explanatory notes – would lead to success. Once again, a change of government led to the end of the tax: first reduced to 60% in 1979, then abolished in 1985.

More modest and adaptable measures adopted in Britain that have had similar effects in maintaining high land prices and choking off supply have been variously called **planning obligations, planning gain** or **Section 106 Agreement** payments. These were introduced in 1971, therefore predate DLT, but have become much more sophisticated as time has passed. They arise from the shared desire of both planning authorities and developers to ensure that the off-site infrastructure necessitated by most development schemes can be funded. They can only be levied in order to 'mitigate harm' that would otherwise result from the development, for example by increasing traffic congestion on local roads or overcrowding in local schools. The generic term for such devices that deal with the costs external to a development that are imposed on its promoters is **Impact Fees**. As the name implies, these require that such impacts are identified and costed before a charge can be levied on the developer whose scheme creates the external impact on facilities to be invested in.

The main flaw of Impact Fees, DLT and their ilk is that they place the entire burden for funding infrastructure upon the sponsors of that new development. They do this usually at the worst time for a developer's cash flow, which tends to discriminate against smaller local developers. As other sources of infrastructure funding have dried up, so have local authorities and other public bodies seeking to finance related projects looked to Planning Gain to meet the need, until the courts have had to intervene and establish reasonable limits. The extent and manner of its use has been notoriously variable and unpredictable between – and even within – individual planning authorities. County councils and other public bodies are highly dependent on the planning authority and half of all planning authorities in 2006 were still failing to use S106 Agreements at all.

In order to make such measures more predictable and dispel the whiff of corrupt 'paying for planning permission', several attempts to impose transparency on the levels of payment and types of infrastructure that qualify to benefit have been made. **Tariffs** were informally promoted by some county councils and implemented by planning authorities with the support of the development industry in the 1990s. The 1997 Labour Government brought forward draft legislation to impose tariffs across the country but withdrew it, fearing a lack of flexibility unless undue complexity accompanied the measure. Some councils, notably Milton Keynes and Ashford, also West Berkshire, have developed their own versions as Supplementary Planning Guidance: it is too early to say if these local initiatives will succeed but they appear not to be facing strong developer resistance.

A major problem with the current system is that areas where the economy is over-heating can get away with high tariffs, obliging developers to substantially cut their profits (and/or design quality) if they want a share of the action, whereas in depressed areas no amount of inducement by the planning authority may attract much needed development. What is needed is a nation-wide method of transferring wealth and development from where it is not needed to where it is. Kate Barker's **Planning Gain Supplement** (PGS) is a well-meaning but misguided idea that attempts to do this. However it undermines a long established principle of Planning Gain, which is that the money extracted from the developer must be used to finance infrastructure necessary and related to the scheme to which it is applied as a Condition or S106 term. Hardly anyone in the development industry has praised the PGS, although most commentators – including opposition politicians – seem glumly resigned to getting it. In the 2007 Budget, after several protracted consultations had indicated widespread opposition to PGS, Gordon Brown announced his intention to proceed with it 'not before 2009' and a Bill to enable preparatory activity was by then already approaching Royal Assent. However there are many technical problems still to resolve, not least being the methods for valuing sites both before and after planning permission is awarded: only the assessed uplift in value will be taxed.

The Liberal Democrat policy of **Green Field Development Tax** (GFDT) targets sites when and where the most obscene unearned land value gains occur and where public opposition to development most needs to be assuaged. But in essence it suffers from the same economic defect as other measures of its type. It fails to distinguish between development on green fields that may be justified because there are no suitable nearby brown fields, and that which really ought to be deterred. It was never clear how GFDT revenue would be transferred between the land-poor authority which needs the money to pay for off-site infrastructure and the nearby authority which needs it to clean up contaminated land – or if that was even the intention.

Capital Gains Tax (CGT) has run alongside all the above measures and has the advantage of being administered largely within the staple tax systems of Income Tax and Corporation Tax. However it also suffers from similar levels of complexity as those taxes and lacks any involvement of local authorities. It applies to all kinds of property although 'roll-over relief' for CGT applies only to certain kinds of real estate transaction and in effect leaves many owners exempt.

Inheritance Tax (IHT) is similar to CGT, except that it applies only to the estate of deceased persons: companies, trusts and other corporate bodies never die. It is, in theory, one of the main means of reducing concentrations of wealth within propertied families. However good tax planning enables most seriously rich people to avoid IHT and it now hits the moderately rich harder than most of their heirs expect.

The latest of these transfer taxes is **Stamp Duty Land Tax** (SDLT) which replaced Stamp Duty in 2004. Stamp Duty was applied to the transfer or 'stamping' of the document that legally transferred ownership and could be avoided by carrying out that administrative act in an offshore tax haven. SDLT attempts to counter this form of tax avoidance by applying to the location of the property and not of the paper transaction. It is distinguished currently by having severely regressive effects at the boundaries between bands where the tax rate changes, because the rate applies to the whole value and not just the increment. This encourages developers and other vendors to use every device to keep prices just below the upper limit of a band, e.g. by making fittings and garages 'extras'.

All transfer taxes were called *'the ultimate anti-market tax'* (Bird and Slack 2002, 64) by Ricardo. They do nothing to stimulate – and everything to suppress, delay and distort – beneficial economic activity. Even IHT fails to stimulate the kind of tax planning that would help the housing market work to the benefit of all: releasing large homes as soon as owners cease to really need them. Their main advantage is ease of collection, since they require no skilled valuation (but merely sight of the certified sales documents) and are applied when money is actually changing hands. Some of them also partially 'internalise the externalities' of development but in these cases (GFDT, Planning Gain, Tariffs, Impact Fees) they fail to equitably share among all beneficiaries the burden of paying for external costs. If the principle of extending these kinds of land tax was followed to its logical conclusion, then only purchasers and builders of new housing development would contribute to investment in schools and hospitals in an area. Surely in fairness all those who benefit (actually or potentially) from a new service ought to pay for it?

The **Land Premium** that applies in Hong Kong (described in an earlier chapter) is a special kind of transfer tax, where the state owns the freehold and is therefore able to negotiate as lessor with prospective lessee developers. In effect the Government holds a land auction every year. Sites are released onto the market with a Development Brief and the prospect of a long (99 years or more) lease. The winner of the auction pays a very large up-front sum in return for undertaking to finance, build and manage the development. Subsequent redevelopment of the land within the lease period is similarly subject to land premium charges. This is less restrictive of the market than other transfer taxes, however it does mean that only developers with very large cash reserves can afford to be the principal players in the market. It also leaves the Government vulnerable to fluctuations in the economic climate: revenue from Land Premium is very irregular.

Similar policies are being used in other Chinese cities, although there the leases tend to be shorter. LVT campaigners in Hong Kong are seeking to annualize the payments, using regular monitoring of rental levels, thereby dealing with both the above problems. However even then, it would take many years for such a 'staged' Land Premium to draw revenue from more than a small part of the total area under leasehold.

Community Land Auctions, which featured in the 2005 Liberal Democrat manifesto, would act on the market in a similar way (Leunig 2007). However only a tiny proportion of the total volume of housing land would come within the scheme and it is not clear how mixed use developments or redevelopments would work, nor where the lower limit on plot size would be set. Would redevelopment of a single family home with large garden as a block of flats[41] have to be subjected to auction? As with all other land taxes mentioned so far in this section, auctions fail to capture any of the ongoing rise in land values beyond the sites undergoing development. If they capture significant amounts of revenue, they have seriously negative effects on the market (unless government is freeholder) and/or the wider economy; if they correct market failures, they cannot raise significant sums. As the title of Dr Leunig's paper suggests, their main benefit is to 'unlock' the store of wealth that the current planning system appropriates to landowners from

41 In some planning authority areas, 40% of new housing occurs on small 'windfall' sites within settlements, not on green field sites allocated in the Local Plan

new housing sites, not to replace current taxes. The theory is that 'NIMBYs' would become 'IMBYs'.[42]

MODERNISED RATES[43]

This set of taxes is based on the age-old principle of the tithe, an annual payment based on wealth. Until 1989 all non-agricultural land in the UK was subject to rating, as the main source of local government revenue. Similar taxes exist in most countries and are what most people in the world think of as 'property taxes': transfer taxes are less common and raise far less revenue overall. Varieties include: Uniform Business Rate; Non-Domestic Rate; Flat Rate; Split Rate; Differentiated Property Tax; BID Levy; Tax Increment Financing; Council Tax; and Vacant Land Tax.

The advantage that all these have over one-off property transfer taxes is that they apply to a whole class of property or land use and are levied annually. Their disadvantage, in the eyes of tax accountants and administrators and some politicians is that they rely on subjective valuation of property and not an objective price, also they are not inherently related to ability to pay and are generally painful to pay – the opposite of 'stealth taxes'. However the pain caused by having a separate tax bill, traditional in the UK, is largely avoidable: like other taxes, they can be collected through the income and corporation tax systems if governments choose. This is done in Sweden, where property taxes are national not local.

Originally property rates were levied on owners, as they still are in almost all countries that maintain registers of land title. Only when landowners became a dominant political force in Britain, in the Middle Ages, did the burden of rates fall on occupiers, since the tax authorities had no way of knowing who the owners were so long as ownership records were not maintained. Between 1086 (Domesday Book) and 1872, when a comprehensive set of parish land records was ordered by Parliament, no such records were made. The British rating system became a tax on occupiers by default, not by design.

42 A 'NIMBY' is someone whose 'green' credentials extend little further than their own neighbourhood: Not In My Back Yard.

43 Use of the word 'rates' implies these are always local taxes, whereas taxes of this kind can also be levied centrally.

In Britain **Non-Domestic Rating** (NDR) continues where the pre-Thatcher rating system left off, having ignored Northern Ireland which continues with rating on all kinds of developed land.[44] The rateable value is defined as:

> *'the rent at which it is estimated the hereditament[45] might reasonably be expected to let from year to year assuming ... a state of reasonable repair, but excluding ... any repairs which a reasonable landlord would consider uneconomic ...'*

In addition to paying the entire rent, tenant's rates and taxes, the occupier is presumed to bear the cost of all repairs to – and insurance for – the fabric of a building that they do not own. By this definition, a property that is allowed to become derelict ceases to be valued, for rating purposes, for the class of use to which it has been assigned under the planning system. This goes some way to explaining dereliction: it pays. Only when the owner can find no occupier does any portion of the rates burden attach to him: for some use classes, there is a reduced rate payable for a limited period on empty properties, then none; for others there is none from the time the tenant vacates. However in his March 2007 Budget, Gordon Brown signaled an intention to end rates relief on empty properties, which was a recommendation of Sir Michael Lyons in his report on Local Government finance that month.

The **Uniform Business Rate** (UBR) is the tax payable in mainland Britain under the NDR system, so called because it is at a uniform rate of 'poundage' within each of England, Scotland and Wales. In Scotland the rating lists are compiled and maintained by Boards of Assessors which are part of local government. HM Revenue and Customs'[46] Valuation Office Agency (VOA) maintains the rating lists for England and Wales: the Department for Communities and Local Government (DCLG, formerly ODPM) and the Welsh Executive

---

44 Changes were made to business rates in Northern Ireland in 2005, to bring them more into line with the rest of UK. For example, until then **no** rates were payable on industrial or empty property. Also the rating of domestic property changed in 2007, with CAMA used for revaluation on a capital basis for the first time.

45 A hereditament is a rateable unit, i.e. a property subject to rating. The rating lists are comprised of rateable values of all hereditaments.

46 Formerly Inland Revenue, now merged with HM Customs & Excise.

respectively set uniform rates each year and pay for VOA to do the valuing. If NDR was set by local authorities themselves there would be no change in VOA's work, although UBR would cease to be 'U'. Councils that are billing authorities (districts and unitaries) currently merely administer the rate collection and notify VOA of any material changes in use of land and property: with UBR councils currently keep none of the money, although Government has recently suggested that part of any increase in UBR revenue attributable to their local regeneration initiatives might be kept. The difference between what is collected within a local authority area and what is returned back to it from the UBR pool may be as much as 10% either way: rich areas lose, poor ones gain. With a localized business rate, principal local authorities would once again set their own rate and retain all revenues collected.

With the British rating system, there is no easy way to collect revenue from unregistered vacant land and derelict properties. The UTF's recommended **Vacant Land Tax** (VLT) would largely overcome this deficiency[47] but VLT would require a separate rating/tax list, as well as a tight definition of 'vacant'. In theory, VLT would achieve the most in terms of urban renewal and finance, with the least electoral risk: having all the benefits of LVT on the land where most revenue is currently being 'lost'. However site valuation is most difficult where there is urban dereliction.[48] The problems of a VLT were set out by supporters of LVT at the time the UTF report came out (Vickers 1999). One can imagine avoidance by commencing redevelopment or partial occupancy of 'vacant' sites just to make them no longer vacant. However it might be possible to devise a crude VLT, as a 'fine' for leaving sites unused and a way of helping finance remediation of sites: a carrot and stick approach to the most blatant examples of urban wasteland. This happens in some US cities, e.g. Philadelphia.

If the UK **BID Levy**, described above, had been based on ownership and not occupation of property, as in North America, this

47 Totally – if and when the Land Registers are completed.

48 The valuation problem could be solved by allowing owners to self-assess for VLT, with the local authority being given CPO powers at this valuation. Owners could alternatively accept the independent valuation by VOA. Negotiation of an intermediate figure would not be allowed.

might have allowed vacant and derelict sites and buildings to be included. 'Smart BIDs' may be allowed if it seems that the BID Levy isn't working, after the Government's review of BID funding. Research among prospective BID members in central Liverpool in 2002 showed that a site-value based BID levy would be popular (Vickers 2003). As it operates now in the handful of BIDs that have formed since 2003, the levy restricts BID operation to trivial activities.

Another American idea for financing urban renewal is **Tax Increment Financing** (TIFs). Here the revenue from an anticipated rise in rateable value within a defined area subjected to redevelopment is hypothecated for a set period towards the cost of investments made there. This future revenue stream is then used as collateral to borrow up-front: when the tax increment arises it goes to the finance company instead of the local authority. The problem with TIF is that there is no revenue left for local authorities to finance other consequential investment they might need: what has been called *'increment for some, excrement for the rest'*. If the developer is also the finance company, the end of the TIF payback period often sees special pleading for a continuing tax rebate.

Flat Rate is what many in North America call their standard property tax, which is always levied at state or local (not federal) level. It isn't the same as the UK rating system, because it is levied on owners and on all types of land (except publicly owned land).[49] If Britain switched from taxing occupiers to taxing owners but didn't differentiate between land and buildings, then it too would have adopted the Flat Rate. A move towards LVT, made easier there because their valuation system differentiates between land and building value already – even where there is a single or 'flat' rate on both – is the **Split Rate** or **Differentiated Property Tax**, which some twenty cities in Pennsylvania use. Split Rate is used in several other countries, such as South Africa. It involves setting a higher rate on the land value element. Split rate shines a spotlight on the quality of the valuation system, because it starts to make the split

49 It is also usually based on assessments of capital values not rental values. Some tax authorities use assessed 'tax values' that are deliberately lower than market value in order to make appeals less likely.

in values matter. Until the separate assessment of land/site values, as distinct from gross or flat values of properties, has gained the trust of ratepayers the move all the way to LVT is problematic. At least ten US states and several Canadian provinces are at various stages of allowing Split Rate to be adopted by municipalities.

Council Tax is unique to Britain. It succeeded the brief disaster of the Community Charge or Poll Tax, which was not based on property values at all. It is fairly unusual to have such distinct property taxes as council tax and rates – one based on capital values, one on annual rental values – side by side in a country and gives problems where there are mixed use sites. It is also very unusual to have a property tax with banding like Council Tax: normally valuations are discrete, i.e. they aim to be precise for each property.

With rating systems, it is necessary to distinguish between the assessed value and the tax rate. If the tax rate is low, it matters little how good the valuations are, because taxpayers only argue when the impact of a tax on their finances is significant. With one-off property taxes, there is less scope for arguing about the tax base, which is usually a real transaction. If a taxpayer dislikes paying a punitive transaction tax, he can avoid doing so by avoiding the act which leads to the transaction. With property rating, taxpayer resistance to a significantly high-yield *ad valorem* tax can be minimized in several ways: modernized, transparent mass assessment; self-assessment; transitional arrangements for payment; and more frequent re-assessment. Ideally a rating system, whether based on land values or gross property values, should use up-to-date mass valuations where possible, self-assessment of more complex properties (with the state reserving the right to acquire the property at the owner's valuation), simple payment methods – perhaps embedding payments within income and corporation tax systems – and an independent appeals system with a minimum dispute range (i.e. you can only appeal if your dispute is over a certain proportion of assessed payment). The English NDR has been costing more on its appeal side in recent years than the cost of re-assessments. There is evidence that it would cost no more and be more acceptable to businesses who pay it if annual revaluations were used.

In summary, the 'land taxes' described above are seen as unworthy of support in themselves as reforms to (or aspects of) the existing tax system when compared to LVT. They are either inimical to LVT or their benefits would be achieved far more effectively by LVT and therefore it seems preferable to seek LVT, albeit by a gradual process. This process will have many of the attributes of these taxes but have a more comprehensive overall set of objectives which none of these taxes can match.

How to do it is the challenge. Various technical and political obstacles are strewn across the path towards LVT in Britain. These will now be charted and the path planned and prepared.

Selling LVT: Pilots and Transition

THERE ARE TWO constituencies that need to be addressed when trying to change any policy: the voting public and the professional special interest groups who have a stake in the particular policy area. For the former, the messages need to be very simple.

There are always people whose livelihood depends to some extent on the status quo: among the professionals, these will include many in senior positions who fear their influence will diminish if the systems which they know well change. Unless the plausible objections of these expert stakeholders have first been addressed by those who seek change, there is little chance of success. To a risk-averse Whitehall establishment, their views always weigh heavily in the balance.

Few policy areas could be more sensitive politically and risky technically than property taxation. As the authors of a recent study of land and property taxes for the World Bank said:

> *'Successful property tax reform ... is seldom easy, usually difficult technically, and often not too rewarding in either revenue or political terms'* (Bird & Slack 2002)

Taxation hits people in the pocket, property is emotive as well – and, to manage LVT, information is required about land ownership, occupation and use which, in Britain, we do not yet have. The technical and political activities of property tax reform must be orchestrated carefully.

Comfort can be drawn from several facts, based on recent research and observed history of LVT:

1 Most people understand and accept the ethical, economic and environmental arguments for LVT when they are presented with them;

2 Where LVT has been introduced, it has never been removed by popular vote;
3 It is possible to ensure – and to demonstrate in advance – that most voters clearly 'win' with LVT, from the outset;
4 Technology has made LVT universally cheaper to explain, introduce and maintain, relative to other reforms of property taxes, than ever before;
5 The essential components for LVT, especially the property data required, are becoming available in Britain in any case;
6 Trials of other taxes and politically sensitive or complex policies are becoming more common;
7 There is more support for LVT among opinion formers in Britain and elsewhere than for almost 100 years.

However there are also some significant technical obstacles:

a Primary legislation is needed, even for trials of LVT;
b Secondary legislation is needed to ensure that land ownership registers for England and Wales are completed;
c A complex new IT system is essential for the administration of the tax, significantly more expensive at the outset than current property tax systems, even if probably cheaper to run.

These problems pale into insignificance compared to the political risks that a government would perceive to exist in embarking on LVT, particularly because the losers include some of the most powerful interest groups, the richest individuals and a growing proportion of low-income home-owning voters who loathe all property taxes. There is no doubt that a high degree of political will is required for LVT to be implemented effectively, nor that there are few if any precedents which national politicians can draw comfort from while many pitfalls obstruct the way. However the risks can be lessened by adopting the following principles from the outset:

- Undertake exhaustive but urgent desk studies before committing to full, comprehensive roll-out of LVT nation-wide;
- Commit firmly to far-reaching but gradual reform, accompanying introduction of LVT with a phased elimination of other taxes

of roughly equal overall yield, yet not abandoning the main ones until teething troubles with LVT are resolved;

- Invite local authorities or devolved administrations to run tax-raising trials, part-funded and coordinated by central government;
- Seek wider policy benefits and commercial spin-offs from the data integration that LVT requires, possibly using the private sector to manage the IT projects;
- Address the most obvious defects of the current tax and land policy systems first (e.g. 'constructive dereliction' in inner cities) if necessary at the expense of tax take;
- Take note of the 'law of unintended consequences' and embed flexibility in system design – but resist calls for permanent exemptions and 'special cases'; however ...
- Deal with the 'Little Old Lady'[50] sensitively – she votes.

Specific actions along the way to full LVT, primarily as a national tax on all classes of land at a single rate – which should be stated from the outset as the aspiration – are as follows:

1 **Make it UK Government policy that LVT is seen as a major part of a significant Tax Shift strategy**, removing taxes on 'good things' like jobs and enterprise by introducing new taxes on 'common wealth' sources such as access rights to renewable natural resources of all kinds. By doing so, the government's own property data holdings would automatically be freed up and the trigger for completing land registers is pulled.[51] Ideally some of the following actions will have already been resolved upon and can immediately be instigated but by removing the apparent embargo on saying 'LVT is a Good Idea' within Government all the pent-up desire in academia and think-tanks to undertake

50 Invariably the hardship potentially suffered by income-poor, asset-rich pensioners is cited by opponents of LVT. In practice this can be addressed. According to research at Warwick University, only 1.5% of properties in Council Tax Bands F-H are occupied by **owners** on 'low/modest income' (Orton 2006, 11).

51 HMLR has no authority to impose retrospective registration on owners and is currently having to offer financial inducements (i.e. lose revenue) to persuade owners to register land title where there is no transaction. The 2001 Land Registration Act allows new 'triggers' for compulsory registration to be created by Ministers: a statement of intent to introduce LVT would trigger completion of the entire Register.

research on LVT will be released. The important thing is that LVT must not be seen as a way to fill a gaping hole in the Government's coffers, because then the Tax Shift argument will have been exposed as a sham and will be much harder to resurrect. Some points that need to be highlighted when making the announcement:

a LVT is extremely hard to evade compared to non-property taxes, so that compliance costs for Government are much reduced;
b Most other taxes have very dysfunctional effects on job creation, the environment and/or wealth distribution – geographically and between generations;
c The unfairness of existing property taxes, especially council tax;
d The way in which LVT achieves equalization between rich and poor areas and hence truly deals with the Balance of Funding as between central and local government;
e LVT as a means of recycling land value increments that result from investment in infrastructure, hence ensuring a better public transport system; and most important ...
f LVT is not just any old 'land tax' and works on the economy quite differently.

2 **Invite local authorities and devolved governments to participate in LVT trials**. These would be preceded by desk studies, similar to those already done in Liverpool, Oxfordshire[52] and Whitstable. They might operate across just a small area, such as a BID. Alternatively they might involve a whole region like Greater London – perhaps called 'The Olympic Levy' and using existing BIDs legislation – or Scotland. The desk studies and trials could be completed within a single Parliament. Central government would fund the costs of associated research, monitoring and co-ordination, also devising the draft Bill necessary to enable

52 The Councils' own report is available from the Lib Dem Group office at Vale of White Horse District Council (Godden 2005). See also this author's report for the Lincoln Institute (Vickers 2006).

revenue raising. But the costs – political and financial – of promoting the reforms locally would be carried by the levels of government that were to receive the LVT revenue. Several aspects would be tested by varying the models used, both in theory (through desk studies) and practice:

a **Methods of valuation:**
   i CAMA vs. discrete site-by-site assessment (probably for residential and commercial areas respectively);
   ii Self-assessed or centrally imposed (by VOA), with the former carrying a power of compulsory purchase by the local authority at the owner's valuation;
   iii Definitions of HABU – with and without 'hope value';

b **LVT-free Allowances**. As with Oxfordshire, a 'Homestead Allowance' for residential property could increase the numbers 'winning' from the Tax Shift.[53] Some have suggested a similar allowance might apply, at least initially, to other kinds of land use or temporary exemption applied to sites under a certain size or value. However all such allowances complicate the reform and dilute its benefits to some other people.

c **Abatement of other local taxes**. Except for BIDs and a special Olympic Levy, which it might be possible to sell to voters as extra revenue for extra expenditure, the Tax Shift principle must be maintained by ensuring revenue-neutral operation of LVT. This could either be by reducing UBR or other central grant revenue to the pilot authorities by the amount raised or – much more likely – by reducing other taxes levied by that level of government by that amount, with a margin of, say, one percent.
   i **In a Smart BID.** The whole of the BID levy would be raised from site values only, with part of the basic UBR abated as well and replaced by SVR levied across all non-residential

53 There are different ways of applying personal wealth allowances, all of which could be tried. It would not be difficult – and would be equitable – for the tax-free allowance to be in proportion to the average house price in a local authority area. The rate currently set for Housing Benefit, meant to be a minimum living standard, could be related to tax-free allowance on LVT.

land, thus making the yield:cost ratio from the new tax greater. Otherwise it would seem scarcely worth the trouble administering SVR just to cover the BID expenditure.

ii **Replacing Council Tax.** All or part of the current council tax revenue replaced by SVR on residential property.

iii **Replacing CT and NDR**. All or part of both CT and NDR replaced by SVR on all non-agricultural land.

3 **Evaluate the costs and benefits of the trials and bring forward legislation for permanent LVT**. Depending on the outcome of the trials and the political climate at the time, it might be decided to implement LVT as a national, regional or local tax – or all three – for all or only certain kinds of land use. Ideally LVT should replace both CT and NDR UK-wide, so as to maximize the yield from the fixed cost of installing new valuation systems. However devolved governments might wish to continue with their own versions of property tax.[54]

4 **Components of a Model Bill for LVT**. Subject to the outcome of trials and evaluation of wider benefits of comprehensive land valuation, Government would bring forward a LVT Bill,[55] the main provisions of which might be as follows.

a Regular (at least bi-annual) valuation of all land, primarily for tax purposes but also as a wider economic and land management policy aid, with all assessments freely available in the public domain;

b A single LVT tax rate at UK level, revenue used to fully replace the 'Barnett money' for revenue equalization between the four nations, with a standard formula for national Homestead Allowance, variable according to local house prices;

c Nations and regions allowed to levy up to the yield equivalent

---

54 Northern Ireland and Scotland already administer property taxes independently of VOA and there is no reason why GLA or the Welsh Executive could not be allowed to administer their own systems, as local authorities did until the 1970s. There are however advantages in keeping the tax assessment system independent from political control by the government that sets the tax rates. Also there are very significant advantages beyond the tax system in having a consistent basis for valuing land: in spatial planning and for the effective working of the property market.

55 Scotland and Northern Ireland would have different provisions.

of, say, 3p/£ (3%) of income tax from LVT,[56] provided selected other taxes are abated. The 'menu' of these other taxes would be drawn up by UK Government and the timetable also set under secondary legislation;

d UBR fully replaced by SVR over a five-year period, with existing rating lists frozen at 2005 levels as nation-wide site valuations of non-domestic land are undertaken;

e Agricultural land (i.e. land subject to CAP regime payments) zero-rated for LVT until the EU reforms CAP – but other rural land (e.g. 'horsiculture'[57] or private amenity land) coming under LVT immediately;

f SDLT, CGT and IHT on real estate transactions abated immediately upon introduction of UK-wide LVT and phased out entirely as the UK-wide LVT rate is raised;

g Planning gain and S106 payments phased out over 5-10 years as SVR is introduced as the main source of revenue for local authorities, replacing council tax as well as NDR;

h A one-year 'freeze' on LVT rates when sites are awarded planning permission, to allow time for land assembly and pre-contract negotiation between owner(s) and developer;[58]

i SVR rates (and possibly additional associated local Homestead Allowance) set by local authorities within a range set by national governments;

j Local authorities allowed to precept central government to

56 The Liberal Democrat proposal to replace Council Tax (which yields about £21bn/yr) with a Local Income Tax equates to about a 3.5% on income tax. The national housing stock is valued at about £3tr, according to the National Institute for Economic & Social Research (NIESR 2007), of which about half is land value (varying from over 75% in Central London to 30% in poorer regions). Therefore a 1% LVT could either replace Council Tax or about 3.5p/£ of income tax.

57 The word is not yet in a conventional dictionary but 'horsiculture' is said in a publication of the Macaulay Land Use Research Institute to be land with 'many horses being grazed outdoors for part of the year ... formerly used for livestock grazing' (Quetier and Gordon 2003)

58 If owners do not accept the official site valuation for the new HABU, their self-assessed value could be accepted – but with the planning authority reserving the right to acquire the freehold at the owner's valuation **and no possibility of negotiating an intermediate valuation**. Alternatively, for the first 2-3 years **after** (re-)development of a site, its total LVT bill could be halved: an incentive to develop where needed and enabling accurate post-development site valuations to be assessed.

raise SVR through national tax systems,[59] enabling billing authorities to either become local offices of IR or to deal direct with IR rather than local taxpayers (except to send out notification of SVR rates);

k Local councils (parishes, communities and towns) also adopt SVR, precepting for residential land only; BIDs similarly use LVT and precept on national government (non-residential land only).

59 This implies that trials of LVT/SVR within the Income Tax and Corporation Tax systems are successful. The model would be that used in two-tier local government areas for rates

Timetable to Full National LVT

DESK STUDIES preceding local tax-raising trials would take only two years. Since no Party has such a programme as described above in its manifesto, it has to be accepted that desk studies are all that could happen before a General Election in 2009-10. An immediate announcement of its intention to introduce LVT by the incoming Government could trigger a national land valuation within six months. The work could be concentrated in limited trial areas with no need for additional Vote expenditure.

Tax-raising local trials could be established within a year but would need three financial years before any assessment of their success could be made and a further two years during which they could continue revenue-raising and refining their systems, under an overall national monitoring programme.

The LVT Bill outlined above could be brought before Parliament within a year of the next General Election and be enacted by 2011, in time for local tax-raising trials. Given the current state of the three main parties, it is quite likely that no one party will have a clear majority in that Parliament. It is therefore sensible to seek an early consensus on the way forward between at least two of those parties, highly desirable to have consensus on the main thrust of the Tax Shift through LVT principle by the middle of the current Parliament.

All three main Westminster parties have significant numbers of advisers and supporters who favour LVT. The Bow Group, a centre-right Conservative Party body with many MPs as members, submitted proposals for a form of LVT to the Forsyth Review of Tax Policy conducted in 2006 (Wadworth 2006). Although these did not make it to the report's recommendations, there are many in the Party who find the free-market angle to LVT attractive. The Labour Land Campaign has more members than for several decades, including at least nine members of the 2001-5 Parliament and John McDonnell, Gordon Brown's would-be challenger as Leader in 2007. The Liberal Democrats re-affirmed their support for LVT at their 2006 Party Conference, by a comfortable majority.

2009, the Centenary Year of the Peoples Budget, would be a good year to publish a draft Bill on LVT. Full UK-wide implementation at all levels of government could be achieved in seven to ten years from the start of desk studies, i.e. by the end of the 2010 Parliament, in 2014/15. A start could be made on nation-wide domestic LVT before the policy's promoters seek a mandate for a substantial Tax Switch off basic general taxes such as income and corporation tax. However it ought to be possible to go into the next General Election with a pledge to replace all existing property taxes with just one, based on site values alone, within a single Parliament.

A further Tax Shift, off taxes on 'goods' like earnings and enterprise, would proceed over the next five years, with LVT yielding at least £50 billion per year (at current values) by 2020.

Postscript: 'Beyond *Terra Firma*'

Other global and local 'commons' to harvest for the Common Good

THIS SECTION gives a flavour of the range of opportunities that exist for modern governments for legitimate revenue raising from 'resource rents'. Most of these opportunities are new and were unknown in the time of Henry George, because it is advances in technology and in society's needs that have created uses for aspects of Nature that were always there. Just as it would have been meaningless to talk of America's land value before Vespucci and Columbus discovered the New World, so too is the economic rent of other natural resources like the electro-magnetic spectrum irrelevant until some human use has been discovered for them.

Spectrum

When Gordon Brown auctioned the right to have exclusive access to certain wavelengths of the broadcast spectrum among suppliers of third generation mobile phone network services, he was capturing the considerable value (£21bn over 20 years) of a renewable natural resource for public benefit. When the US Federal Government allows Rupert Murdoch free access to other wavelengths so his companies can broadcast to American citizens, it is giving something away which is worth a fortune but would have no value if those citizens were without spending power to consume the products of American enterprise.

In countries where the demand for access to the broadcast spectrum and the population density are high, the price that could be achieved at auction is much higher than in a sparsely populated country with neither desire nor ability to exploit modern mobile telecommunications, broadcasting or mass consumer spending. It is a case of a natural resource only being valuable because society as a whole, in that general area, has created a need and a value for the right to access that resource. States should not just allocate these finite resources, they should charge the licensees what the market will pay for the right of exclusive access to them. Otherwise the economic rent, which is Common Wealth, goes by default to the licensees in its entirety.

Temporary exclusive rights

The same applies to the humble parking meter. There is no point in charging for parking beside a freeway crossing a desert. Society has created a space in the public domain but the value of that space depends on the competition to occupy it. As with land sites, unless you create more space in the vertical dimension, there is a limit to the amount that can be provided for cars at the roadside.

Moving into that vertical dimension, by air, requires a landing on *terra firma* somewhere. Analogous to the parking meter is the aircraft landing slot. Peak commuter morning and early evening slots at Heathrow are worth more than at Prestwick, which are worth more than at a provincial airstrip in Nepal. John Prescott was quite right to press for an auction of landing slots, instead of leaving British Airways to sub-let its high-value slots to the benefit of its shareholders. It is the relative prosperity of south east England as a whole that creates the extra value, not the airline.

Over and under

As urban living becomes more complex, we need to consider land rent in three dimensions. Traditional 'land rights' assume that the person holding title to a land site 'owns' everything from the centre of the earth to outer space within a projected terrestrial area – an irregular cone. In cities with subways and multi-level malls, the term 'air rights' is becoming common in property law and the two dimensional approach breaks down. Governments need to manage the physical space of their domains three dimensionally, allocating space in geodetic terms.

Far out

Ultimately, as the private sector ventures into space exploration, orbits around Earth should be rented out – but by whom? This, as is the case with Antarctica by Treaty– and for the deep sea – is in theory already possible, although the institutions for governance and especially for handling revenue and deciding who spends it on what are fragile. The value is potentially highly significant but perhaps more important is the authority that would accompany the creation of a global institution able to manage the resources of these ill-defined Commons.

Nature that moves

So long as nobody has secure legal title to a resource, there is no incentive to exploit it sustainably: the 'slash and burn' culture will continue. Naked power of possession is a poor recipe for sustainable management of scarce resources, whether renewable or not.

Some Global Commons are movable, although their origins may be geographically defined. Rare plants have traditional uses among aboriginal peoples but are then 'discovered' and removed to a distant laboratory. Should the natural qualities of those plants become 'owned' by a drug company? Or should their genetic code be licensed by some global authority to companies, perhaps by auction or by periodic revaluation of their commercial potential? Should part of the revenue from such licence fees be recycled back to conserve the natural environment from which the plant originally came? These are questions whose answers should be guided by the theory of economic rent. If something is not created by humankind but is merely discovered, its inherent value is our Common Wealth.

Fish and bird stocks move, whether we like it or not. Would not the principle of resource rents as revenue help in their management? Clearly no single country can adequately manage such natural resources. The EU fishing policy is widely regarded as a failure. Ironically it was the Soviet fishing fleet which may have established a more sustainable model for managing this kind of resource.

Seigneurage

A vital and intriguing piece in the puzzle of where to define the boundaries of rent as revenue is money itself. Is not the power to create money something that could be regarded as a function of the sophistication of society, of its ability to produce and spend? By allowing banks to create money, governments have also allowed their currencies to be debased. The potential to create wealth for private lenders – rather than for the public as a whole – from the need of society to have a means of exchange of value in goods and services, known as *seigneurity* in earlier times, could be regarded as proportionate to the size and economic capacity of a society. Little money can be made from lending to an aboriginal tribe, much more from lending to the entire British population.

Humanity is part of Nature. On a shoulder bag for sale in the tiny 'Georgist' township of Arden, Delaware I saw perhaps the profoundest words of the man who inspired so many reformers of a hundred years ago: 'There is, in Nature, no reason for Poverty.' Could it be that in our monetary system itself lies the seed of our species' downfall? As Henry George saw then, in the middle of apparent economic progress we continue to tolerate extreme global poverty. Robertson, Rowbotham, Braund and others quoted here have suggested that the Land Question may have morphed into the Money Question: so much 'money' is backed ever more tenuously by landed wealth that should be our Common Wealth, used to restore economic and social justice within a free market. Better minds than mine will need to explore this further.

For now – not tomorrow but **now** – I would urge the reader to consider my proposals for recycling Britain's Common Wealth: a practical and urgent matter for modern politicians and property professionals alike and together.

Glossary

AFM	Alternative Funding Mechanism
AGI	Association for Geographic Information
ALTER	Action on Land-value Taxation and Economic Reform. A campaign group within the Liberal Democrat Party.
AREIS	Assessors Real Estate Information System
AVM	Automated Valuation Method
BID	Business Improvement District
CAMA	Computer Aided Mass Assessment. Application of automated valuation techniques to tax administration.
CAP	Common Agricultural Policy
CGT	Capital Gains Tax
C-SCAIPE	Centre for Sustainable Communities Achieved through Integrated Professional Education
CT	Council tax
DCLG	Department for Communities and Local Government
DLT	Development Land Tax
EC	European Commission
ECMT	European Committee of Ministers of Transport
EU	European Union
EUV	Existing Use Value
FoE	Friends of the Earth
GDP	Gross Domestic Product
GFDT	Green Field Development Tax
GIS	Geographic Information Systems
GLC	Greater London Council. Abolished in 1986, replaced by Greater London Authority in 1999.
GWR	Geographically weighted regression
HABU	Highest and best use
HGF	Henry George Foundation

HMLR	Her Majesty's Land Registry, covering England & Wales only.
IHT	Inheritance Tax
INSPIRE	INfrastructure of SPatial InfoRmation on the Environment
IR	Inland Revenue, now Her Majesty's Revenues and Customs (HMRC).
IRRV	Institute for Revenues Rating and Valuation. The professional body to which all involved with property taxes belong.
IVSC	International Valuation Standards Committee
JLE	Jubilee Line Extension of the London Underground railway
JRF	Joseph Rowntree Foundation
LVT	Land Value Taxation
LVTC	Land Value Taxation Campaign. A non-party group which focuses on informing UK Parliamentarians.
MEP	Member of the European Parliament
MSP	Member of the Scottish Parliament
NDR	Non-domestic rating
NEF	New Economics Forum
NIMBY	Not in my back yard
ODPM	Office of the Deputy Prime Minister (predecessor to DCLG).
OS	Ordnance Survey
PA	Pennsylvania
PAYE	Pay as you earn
PF	Progressive Forum
QUANGO	Quasi-autonomous non-governmental organisation
RSA	Rating Surveyors Association
SDLT	Stamp Duty Land Tax
SVR	Site Value Rating
TCPA	Town and Country Planning Association
TfL	Transport for London
TIF	Tax Increment Financing
UBR	Uniform Business Rate
UTF	Urban Task Force
VAT	Value Added Tax
VLT	Vacant Land Tax
VOA	Valuation Office Agency

References and Selected Bibliography

A Economic and taxation theory

Banks, R. (2001) *Double-cross*. London: Centre for Land Policy Studies.

Braund, M. (2005) *The Possibility of Progress*. London: Shepheard-Walwyn.

Dale, P., Mahoney, R. & McLaren, R. (2002) 'Land Markets and the Modern Economy.' Paper in Leading Edge Series. RICS.

Gaffney, M. (1998) 'Red-light Taxes and Green-light Taxes.' Paper presented at *Sharing our Common Heritage: Resource taxes and green dividends*, Conference at Oxford, 14 May 1998 (published at http://www.jamesrobertson.com/book/sharingourcommonheritage.pdf).

Gaffney, M. & Harrison, F. (1994) *The Corruption of Economics*. London: Shepheard-Walwyn.

George, H. (1879) *Progress and Poverty*. Edited and abridged by Bob Drake, 2006. 310pp. New York: Robert Schalkenbach Foundation.

Giacalone, J. & Cobb, C. (2001) *The Path to Justice: Following in the footsteps of Henry George*. Malden, MA, USA: Blackwell Publishing.

Gloudemans, R.J. (2002) 'An Empirical Analysis of the Incidence of Location on Land and Building Values.' Working Paper 02RG1. Cambridge, MA, USA: Lincoln Institute of Land Policy.

Harrison, F. (2005) *Boom Bust: House prices, banking and the depression of 2010*. London: Shepheard-Walwyn.

Harrison F. (2006) *Ricardo's Law: House prices and the great tax clawback scam*. London: Shepheard-Walwyn.

Huhne, C. (1990) *Real World Economics*. London: Penguin Books.

Leunig, T. (2007) 'In My Back Yard: Unlocking the planning system.' Policy Paper for Centre Forum.

Lichfield, N. & Connellan, O. (2000) 'LVT and Eco-taxation: Their social and economic inter-relationship.' Working Paper WP00NL4. Cambridge, MA, USA: Lincoln Institute of Land Policy.

Muellbauer, J. (2003) 'Housing, Credit and the Euro: The policy response.' Paper for HM Treasury (www.housingoutlook.co.uk/Papers/outlook.pdf).

Quetier, F.F. & Gordon, I.J. (2003) '"Horsiculture": How important a land use change in Scotland?' *Scottish Geographic Journal* 119:2, pp.153-8. Aberdeen: Macaulay Land Use Research Institute.

Robertson, J. (1994) 'Benefits and Taxes: A radical strategy.' A discussion paper. London: New Economics Foundation.

Robertson, J. (1998) *Beyond the Dependency Culture*. London: Adamantine Press.

Robertson, J. (1999) *The New Economics of Sustainable Development: A briefing for policy makers*. London: Kogan Page.

Rowbotham, M. (2002) *Goodbye America! Globalisation, debt and the dollar empire*. London: Carpenter.

Smith, A. (1776) *An Inquiry into the Nature and Causes of the Wealth of Nations*. Bk.5, Ch.2, Pt.2, Art.1 (re-published at http://oll.libertyfund.org/ToC/0141-03.php).

Vickers, A., Sayce, S., Connellan, O. & Morad, M. (2005) 'A Revealing Landvaluescape: Making property tax more acceptable using value maps.' In *Critical Issues in Environmental Taxation: International & comparative perspectives*, Volume III. Cavaliere, A. *et al* (eds) 2006, pp.565-90. London: Richmond Law & Tax.

B Property and land taxes UK

Blundell, V. (1993) *Essays in Land Economics*. London: Economic & Social Science Research Association.

Burt, P. (2006) *Report of the Local Government Finance Review Committee*. Scottish Parliament (http://www.localgovernmentfinancereview.org/report/report.aspx).

Connellan, O. (2004) *Land Value Taxation in Britain: Experience and opportunities*. Cambridge, MA, USA: Lincoln Institute of Land Policy.

Craig, J. (2004) 'The New Capital Adequacy Directive: RICS response.' Open letter to HM Treasury from RICS, 9 March 2004.

Dixon, T. (2001) *Business Rates 2000*. London: Institute of Revenues, Rating & Valuation.

Godden, M., Ashton-Kane, R.J.I., Bizzell, P., Black, J., Hodgson, B., Simmons, C. & Vickers, A.J.M. (2005) *The Oxfordshire Land Value Tax Study*. Oxfordshire County Council, January 2005.

Heard, J. (2005) 'Troubled Waters.' In *Valuer*, March 2005, p.16.

Hinnells, M. & Potter, S. (2001) 'Don't Tax More, Tax Different!' Paper No.20. London: Centre for Reform.

Jacobs, M. (2000) *Paying for Progress: A new politics of tax for public spending*. Report of the Commission on Taxation and Citizenship. London: Fabian Society.

KPMG (1999) 'Fiscal Incentives for Urban Housing.' Paper for the Urban Task Force. London: The Stationery Office.

Liberal Democrat Party (2000) 'Engaging Communities.' Policy Paper 37.

Liberal Democrat Party (2006) 'Fairer, Simpler, Greener.' Policy Paper 75.

Lyons, M. (2007) 'Place-shaping: A shared ambition for local government.' Final Report of the Lyons Inquiry into Local Government (www.lyonsinquiry.org.uk).

Maxwell, D. & Vigor, A. (eds) (2005) *Time for Land Value Tax?* Oxford: Institute of Public Policy Research.

McGill, G. & Plimmer, F. (2004) 'An Examination into the Effects of LVT in the UK: An update of the Whitstable Case Studies.' Working Paper. Cambridge, MA, USA: Lincoln Institute of Land Policy (http://www.lincolninst.edu/pubs/pub-detail.asp?id=922).

McLean, I. (2005) *The Fiscal Crisis of the United Kingdom*. London: Palgrave.

Muellbauer, J. (2004) 'Property and Land, Taxation and the Economy.' Paper for Joseph Rowntree Foundation.

NIESR (2007) 'Taxation of Housing'. A presentation by Martin Weale, Director NIESR, at a conference *Smart Taxes replacing Bad Taxes: If not now then when?* 15 May 2007. Waterfront Conference Company.

ODPM (2004a) *Balance of Funding Review – Report*. London: ODPM.

Orton, M. (2006) 'Struggling to Pay Council Tax: A new perspective on the debate about local taxation.' Paper for Joseph Rowntree Foundation.

Pickard, D. (2004) *Lie of the Land*. London: Land Research Trust.

RICS (2004) *Land Value and Public Transport*. London: RICS.

Riley, D. (2001) *Taken for a Ride*. London: Centre for Land Policy Studies.

Rogers, R. *et al* (1999) *Towards an Urban Renaissance*. Report of the Urban Task Force. London: E. & F. Spon.

Roy, R. (2004) 'Not by Spending Alone: The case for a comprehensive tax review.' The Railway Forum (http://www.railwayforum.com/publications.php?year=2004).

Vickers, A.J.M. (1999) 'Paying for Urban Renewal.' Paper for Henry George Foundation.

Vickers, A.J.M. (2003) 'A Blueprint for Smart Tax in Britain.' Working Paper. Cambridge, MA, USA: Lincoln Institute of Land Policy (http://www.lincolninst.edu/pubs/pub-detail.asp?id=861).

Vickers, A.J.M. (2006) 'Landvaluescape and UK Tax Reform: A report on aspects of the study of land value taxation carried out in Oxfordshire 2003-5.' Working Paper. Cambridge, MA, USA: Lincoln Institute of Land Policy (http://www.lincolninst.edu/pubs/PubDetail.aspx?pubid=1109).

Wadsworth, M. (2006) 'Tax, Benefits, Pensions.' Paper for Conservative Party Tax Reform Commission, Bow Group.

Whelan, J. (2003) *Funding London's Transport Needs*. London: RICS.

C Property and land taxes overseas

Aleksiene, A. & Bagdonavicius, A. (2006) 'Lessons in Introducing Value-Based Property Taxes in Lithuania.' Paper for *Making the Property Tax Work in the Developing World*, due publication 2007 by Lincoln Institute of Land Policy.

Andelson, R. *et al* (2000) *Land-Value Taxation Around the World*, third edition. Malden, MA, USA: Blackwell Publishing.

Bird, R.M. & Slack, E. (2002) 'Land and Property Taxation Around the World: A review.' In *Journal of Property Tax Assessment & Administration* 7(3), 31-80.

Brisbane City Council (1989) *Report of the Commission of Inquiry into Valuation and Rating* (http://www.landvaluetax.org.uk/brisbane.htm).

City of Harrisburg (2006) 'City of Harrisburg Two-tier Tax Rate.' Collection of documents produced by Mayor's office in response to regular inquiries on the subject.

Durning, J.T. & Bauman, Y. (1998) *Tax Shift*. Seattle: North West Environment Watch.

ECMT (2003) *Reforming Transport Taxes*. Paris: CEMT (http://www.cemt.org/topics/taxes/taxpub.htm).

? Bill McCluskey? BFS NI

Franzsen, R.C.D. & McCluskey, W.J. (2005) 'An Exploratory Overview of Property Taxation in the Commonwealth of Nations.' Working Paper. Cambridge, MA, USA: Lincoln Institute of Land Policy.

Josten, R. (2001) 'Land Value Rating: A possibility to reform the German property rates.' In *Journal of Property Tax Assessment & Administration*, 6(3), 63

Lichfield, N. & Connellan, O. (2000) 'LVT for the Benefit of the Community: A review of the current situation in the EU.' Working Paper WP00NL3. Cambridge, MA, USA: Lincoln Institute of Land Policy.

Ó Siochrú, E. (2004) 'Land Value Tax: Unfinished business.' Foundation for the Economics of Sustainability (FEASTA). Accessed 15 April 2005 at http://www.feasta.org/documents/landhousing/coritax.html#f23.

Plassman, F. & Tideman, N. (1999) 'A Markov Chain Monte-Carlo Analysis of the Effect of Two-Rate Property Taxes on Construction.' In *Journal of Urban Economics* 47(2), 216-47.

Shaefer, S. (2004) 'Russia: Reforming the Reformers. An interview with Michael Hudson by Standard Shaefer.' In *CounterPunch* 27 Feb 2004 at http://www.counterpunch.org/schaefer02272004.html.

UN-HABITAT (2006) 'Terms of Reference for the Development of GLTN Tool on Land Value Taxation.' Contract document issued 1 Nov 2006 to Earth Rights Institute.

Ward, R., Guilford, J., Jones, B., Pratt, D. & German, J. (2002) 'Piecing Together Location: Three studies by the Lucas County R&D Section.' *Assessment Journal* September/October 2002, p.21.

D Websites

www.1909.org Planning for the centenary of Lloyd George's 'Peoples Budget'

www.cooperativeindividualism.org School of Cooperative Individualism (American Libertarians)

www.c-scaipe.ac.uk Centre for Sustainable Communities Achieved through Integrated Professional Education

www.earthrights.net Earth Rights Institute, working with UN-HABITAT on LVT

www.gltn.net UN HABITAT's Global Land Tools Network (online resource for land reformers)

www.henrygeorge.org Online free education in Classical Georgist economics

www.interunion.org.uk International Georgist Union (UK-based UN ECOSOC)

www.labourland.org.uk Labour Party LVT campaign group

www.landvaluescape.org Land Value Mapping research

www.landvaluetax.org.uk The Land Value Taxation Campaign, a non-party lobby group

www.libdemsalter.org.uk Liberal Democrat LVT campaign group

www.lincolninst.edu Lincoln Institute of Land Policy, Cambridge, MA, USA

www.lvrg.org.au Land Values Research Group, Australian group researching economic rents

www.progress.org American network for 'Economic Justice Network', very active site with wide-ranging interests